Albert Einstein is reported to have [said everything] should be made as simple as pos[sible...] Jeff Johnson has meticulously followed that counsel in this book. With the competence of a careful student and the heart of a faithful pastor, he has done the hard work of investigating the origins, development, and wickedness of the modern social justice movement. Well-researched, clearly written, and necessarily succinct, *What Every Christian Needs to Know about Social Justice* will be the first book I recommend to believers who want a trustworthy introduction to that movement.

– **Thomas Ascol**
Pastor, Grace Baptist Church, Cape Coral, FL;
President, Founders Ministries

The social justice agenda is a perverse movement that has various tentacles that impact nearly all the spheres of our modern society, including political, economic, academic, medical, athletic, and most troubling of all—the church of Jesus Christ. Due to the vast diversity and complexity of the movement, it becomes a unique challenge to explain the dangers of social justice. Jeff Johnson, in his book *What Every Christian Needs to Know about Social Justice*, fulfills the calling of a Christian by contending "for the faith that was once for all delivered to the saints" (Jude 3). Make no mistake about it, the social justice agenda is a devilish agenda, and Jeff Johnson explains and exposes it in his helpful book.

– **Josh Buice**
Pastor, Pray's Mill Baptist Church, Douglasville, GA;
Founder and president of G3 Ministries

With concise precision, Jeffrey Johnson exposes the treacherous foundation of social justice, revealing the risk to society as a whole and, more importantly, the terrible danger for God's people who offer any credence to it. Johnson exhibits for the reader the detrimental effects of this dangerous ideology from its formalized inception until today, pointing out that what is called social justice is not justice at all. The only lens through which to accurately access the injustices in our world is the Bible. Social justice lacks the proper foundation to be able to provide the exclusive solution of Christ's gospel. Only this good news will suffice in a world filled with injustices.

– Anthony Mathenia
Pastor, Christ Church, Christiansburg, VA

Every Christian is required by God to "do justice" (Mic. 6:8). With our Bibles full of exhortations to do and love justice, what are Christians to make of the social justice movement? My fear, as a pastor, is that many Christians confuse the social justice movement with the Bible's calls to do justice. They are not the same. The social justice movement is a stage-four cancer that has metastasized to the church. Pastor Jeff Johnson helps the Christian to understand the worldview of the social justice movement, as well as its profound deficiencies, indeed, its injustices. Jeff's book is a clarion call to discern this movement and see it for what it is. With his typical clarity, he has given the church a brief, to-the-point handbook that every Christian should read.

– Brian Borgman
Founding pastor, Grace Community Church, Minden, NV

Jeff Johnson has given us a clear, doctrinally sound, historically astute, and philosophically insightful account of the development of critical theory and its manifestation in the social justice movement. From the frank admission of Marxism by BLM, Jeff traces out the subtle developments from that original epistemological positivism expressed as atheistic materialism to today's deconstruction of society and hostility to the faith, ontology, and worldview of the Bible. Only a destruction of the spheres of individual freedom, family unity, state stability, and church liberty will clear the path for the vision of a rebuilt society on terms acceptable to the proponents of social justice theory. Eliminate so-called oppression through a genuinely intolerant oppression. Read this book; absorb its analysis, get in tune with its reasoning, and embrace its robust God-centered, Bible-centered, and gospel-centered understanding of humanity, the world, and a truly just society.

– Tom J. Nettles

Definitions are important, and perhaps no more so than with a biblical understanding of justice. Jeff Johnson has done Christians a great service by helping to show how contemporary definitions of social justice differ from what the Bible teaches about justice. I hope churches use this resource to help believers understand the difference.

– Scott Aniol
Associate professor and
director of doctoral worship studies,
Southwestern Baptist Theological Seminary

In the last forty years, the church has faced threats to the gospel that demand us to "rightly divide" the Scriptures so that we can hear the voice of Christ with clarity in each theological battle. Today there is a looming threat to the gospel that is potentially greater than anything the modern church has previously seen. This threat is critical theory and its spawn, social justice, which is rooted in Marxism.

What makes this so dangerous is that many who were once trusted voices for theological fidelity have been taken captive by this worldly ideology. Paul's warning should ring in our ears to beware worldly "philosophy and empty deception" that is based in the "tradition of men, according to the elementary principles of the world, rather than according to Christ" (Col. 2:8).

One problem in this current battle is that this enemy is not easily defined. The topics of Marxism, critical theory, and social justice are complex and can be confusing to the average person. This is why I commend Jeffrey Johnson's book *What Every Christian Needs to Know about Social Justice*.

With great precision, Dr. Johnson rightly defines and explains the origins and dangers of social justice in a way that neither overstates the problem nor understates the danger. For some time, I have longed for a book to be written that would help pastors and congregants to understand these complex issues and know how to respond biblically. That book has finally arrived!

– **Tom Buck**
Senior pastor, First Baptist Church, Lindale, TX

We have great need for clarity on the matter of justice. Nearly everywhere you look you can see confusion over what justice is and how we might do it. Our ethical confusion stems from a problem down below. Christians desperately need someone to clearly and succinctly show the true nature of our justice problems. Jeff Johnson has provided just the resource we need. He gets down to the root of the matter, demonstrating that there is no compatibility between social justice and true justice. Jeff gets down to the origins and details the incompatibility of the methods of social justice and true justice. This book will help you think clearly about social justice, see its incompatibility with Christianity, and lay a foundation from which you can lovingly and courageously "do justice, love kindness, and walk humbly with your God" (Micah 6:8).

–Jared Longshore
Associate pastor, Grace Baptist Church, Cape Coral, FL;
Vice-president, Founders Ministries

The blinding speed with which the so-called social justice movement has fundamentally transformed Western culture has left most Christians asking, "What happened, and is it too late for me to even try to understand?" A bunch of books are appearing with strange names like Foucault and Derrida splashed across the pages, and many are left more confused than ever by attempting to read them. Jeff Johnson has done us a great favor by sticking to the key issues and shining a bright light on the destructive impact of this highly irrational, anti-human, and very much anti-Christian movement that has taken over our public institutions and the minds of many of our fellow citizens.

– James White
Director of Alpha and Omega Ministries

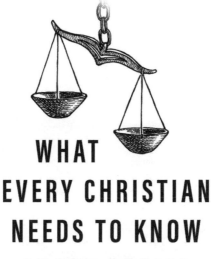

WHAT
EVERY CHRISTIAN
NEEDS TO KNOW
ABOUT SOCIAL
JUSTICE

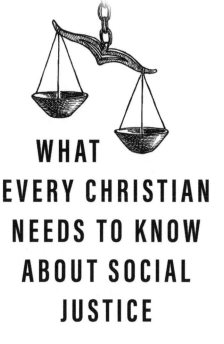

WHAT
EVERY CHRISTIAN
NEEDS TO KNOW
ABOUT SOCIAL
JUSTICE

JEFFREY D. JOHNSON

FREE GRACE PRESS

What Every Christian Needs to Know about Social Justice
Copyright © 2021 by Jeffrey D. Johnson

Published by Free Grace Press
1076 Harkrider
Conway, AR 72032
freegracepress.com

Cover design by Scott Schaller

ISBN:
978-1-952599-27-9 (paperback)
978-1-952599-28-6 (ebook)

CONTENTS

Dedicated to

Voddie Baucham

FOREWORD

Social justice is not just *not the gospel.* It is *anti-gospel.*

It is anti-gospel in its principles and its finished convictions; it is anti-gospel in its presuppositions and its animating biases. Jeff Johnson's *tour de force* survey focuses its firepower primarily (though by no means exclusively) on the second area. Karl Marx emerges as the man who, with Engels to carry his water, wished for nothing less than to deconstruct the order God made. Marx hated Fatherly authority. (He was himself a scandalous father who neglected his offspring, who sired a child out of wedlock by his own design and never acknowledged him, as Paul Johnson has shown in his seminal book *Intellectuals.*[1]) He hated divinely

---

1 Paul Johnson, *Intellectuals: from Marx and Tolstoy to Sartre and Chomsky* (New York: Harper Perennial, 1988), 79–80.

formed institutions. He took a long look at creation order, sizing up its glory-tinged dimensions, and then sent into the world *The Communist Manifesto*, a "scholarly" wet bomb designed for one purpose: to destroy what God made.

Marx and Engels's work had real consequences in its day—terrible consequences. But institutions, especially personal ones, are stubborn things. So, the individual, family, state, and church survived—each battered but alive. Then, following some years of positivist dominance (even the positivists, it seems, were confused about positivism), came critical theory, a Marxist-derived attempt to attack not only institutions but the real world, the language and reason and morality required for humans to exist meaningfully. None such elements were valuable in themselves; they were all tools of power, fashioned for oppression, wielded wickedly and unwittingly by ordinary folks who transmitted a regime of enslavement that only intellectuals gifted in the art of resenting all that had shaped and nurtured them could overthrow.

So came the anti-Western Westernites. Making very good money in schools or lecture halls, they carved out nice careers for themselves teaching traditional youth to despise their birthright. But all this stayed in esoteric environs until critical theory was applied to race. Here is a new cultural turning.

The woke have made hay by looking back at real and awful failings like slavery and Jim Crow ideology of the past and arguing that the "white supremacy" that animated such evils is just as operative today, albeit not in neo-Nazis but in ordinary citizens who do not even know they are so tainted.

In response to this poison, we who oppose "racism" and partiality in any form know that sins of partiality must surely be fought by all of us, for the price of liberty is eternal vigilance. Yet we also know that America has made real progress on such matters, that the past must be handled with great care and that the gospel of Christ unifies through the objective accomplishment of atonement and the gift of regeneration (Rom. 6; Eph. 2:11–22; 1 Cor. 6:9–11). Such material, however, is not what woke voices are offering us.

So now cometh the fire. In our day, in the age of "social justice," America must be burned to be cleansed. "White" members of this society must embrace their inherent pigmentation-derived condemnation in order for the civilization to be free; they should "be less white," as Robin DiAngelo (a "white" person) actually urged in a recent training session.[2] Our corporations should pay $75,000 for a hour-long seminar to hear that there is no actual

---

2 Robin DiAngelo, "Confronting Racism, with Robin DiAngelo," LinkedIn Learning (via Archive.Today), accessed February 24, 2021, https://archive.is/W2d3a.

cure for racism—one can only become an "anti-racist" and both denounce and despise oneself. While this project of "social justice" is driven, as Roger Scruton has observed, by "resentment of those who control things," it is—irony of ironies—endlessly, relentlessly seeking control of things, though few comprehend this twisted plan as it unfolds in society.[3]

All this bodes ill, terribly ill, for the church. Wolves, "fierce wolves," will enter it if they can (Acts 20:29). We who love Christ's body must sit up and take notice; we must protect and warn the sheep who are confronting "social justice" differently in our time. Today, many Christians, as I argue in *Christianity & Wokeness*, are quite *confused* about wokeness and "social justice" and understandably so. Still others are *engaged* but tentative, wanting to promote justice but not certain as to whether they should do so through the lens of critical race theory (their suspicions are extremely well-founded, as this book shows in spades). A third group has enthusiastically *embraced* wokeness, is calling "white" people to "repent of white supremacy," and is in real and grave danger of swapping out biblical Christianity for a compromised version of the same.

Which is why it is time to learn from Jeff Johnson, an expert theologian, compassionate churchman,

---

3 Roger Scruton, *Fools, Frauds, and Firebrands: Thinkers of the New Left* (London: Bloomsbury, 2015), 13.

and piercing critic. Because he loves Christ's blood-bought people, Johnson digs deep into the roots of social justice, giving us the definitive accessible overview of this ideology. Readers will come away not only instructed through Johnson's elegant and precisionist prose but thoroughly trained to spot a counterfeit—and social justice is nothing if not a counterfeit. Johnson speaks the truth in love, which is just what the doctor ordered, and the one sure hope of confused, engaged, and wandering men and women alike. Christianity is, after all, a teaching enterprise, grounded in proclamation of the truth and clear thinking, and we have a harvest of truth and clarity in this text.

In the end, we see in these pages that there is a better faith than the replacement religion of social justice. It is the faith grounded in Christ. It is the faith that honors and celebrates creation order. It is the faith that seeks not the detonation of God-made institutions but their spiritual re-enchantment. This is the faith we preach; this is the God we proclaim; this is the gospel—not merely a *different* gospel than wokeness but the *only* gospel there is—in which we glory.

– Dr. Owen Strachan, author,
Christianity & Wokeness (forthcoming, Salem Books),
Reenchanting Humanity: A Theology of Mankind (Mentor);
professor, Midwestern Seminary

INTRODUCTION

At first glance, it appears that social justice and Christianity have a lot in common. They seem to share a few mutual concerns: they're both opposed to bigotry, racism, and oppression; they are mutually concerned for the needy, the afflicted, and the less fortunate within society; and they both seek to resolve conflict as they aspire after unity and peace. And with these shared concerns, it is tempting for Christians (and those who hold to traditional values) to buy into the validity of social justice. I don't know of any Christian who wants to be charged with racism or indifference to the needs of others nor believes racial tension and oppression are desirable.

Yet, social justice is incompatible with Christianity because it is incompatible with natural revelation.

Sharing common concerns does not mean that Christianity and social justice are based on the same foundation or agree on how to reach their stated objectives of justice and equality.

First, as we shall see in the next two chapters, Christianity and social justice have

natural revelation

the knowledge that God communicates to man about Himself through nature that is universally and immediately understood by all

antithetical starting points. Christianity is founded on the core presuppositions that there is a God who has communicated to us what is right and wrong. Social justice, on the other hand, is founded in worldviews—Marxism and critical theory—that outright reject that basic truth.

Second, as we'll demonstrate in chapters 4 and 5, Christianity and social justice have contradictory methods of reaching their stated objectives. Though they may both desire some form of utopia (i.e., heaven), where social and personal conflicts and injustices are eradicated, only Christianity has the power to bring about true peace in a world of diversity.

Social justice is utterly incapable of achieving its objectives. Rather than creating equality, equity, unity, and peace, it only has the power to generate more inequality, inequity, disunity, and conflict.

Regardless of its stated goals, its fruit is ever-increasing injustice and division within society, for you can't expect to end with justice when you begin by rejecting God's law as the authority of what is right and wrong.

As we shall seek to demonstrate, if advocates of social justice are free to carry out their activism to its natural and logical conclusion, they will destroy justice and peace altogether. Social justice seeks to destroy individual rights and the authority of the nuclear family and the conservative church by placing civil authority in the place of God. This is because rebellion against God's authority is at the heart of the social justice movement.

1

THE FOUNDATION OF TRUE JUSTICE

Though a fresh coat of paint may help sell your home, new paint is not essential to the structural integrity of a house. It's not the color on the Sheetrock but the sturdiness of the studs behind that Sheetrock that is vital. A crack in a wall is more easily repaired than a crack in the foundation. In other words, if a house's foundation has shifted or the framing has been eaten up with termites, then its aesthetics really do not matter. Without a strong foundation and a sound infrastructure, it is simply a matter of time before the house collapses.

Likewise, our society cannot continue without a sure foundation and a solid infrastructure. The structural integrity of any society is rooted in its foundation. But what is that foundation? What holds society together? What keeps all the parts and pieces of society from collapsing into chaos?

If we are going to have a rational discussion about societal injustices and racism and oppression, do we not first need to answer these basic questions? How is a society supposed to function? How do we determine the foundation for justice? Can we even begin debating the claims of social justice if we haven't settled on whose authority determines what is just and unjust?

In other words, before we consider what color we should paint the walls, we need to be sure we are actually looking at the same building. And before we argue about privilege and skin color, we need to understand the rules we are playing by. We need to establish upon whose authority we are basing our position.

We are mistaken if we think this is merely a discussion about skin color or privilege or what we should do about statues. These are merely the current symptoms of our society's illness. This conflict descends to the bedrock of our worldview.

As Christians we profess our authority to be God, and it is God who determines what is just and unjust.

It was He in His ultimate wisdom and authority who laid the foundation for society and erected its infrastructure. However, the foundation of social justice is rooted in atheism and relativism. Social justice grew out of Marxism and critical theory, which have foundations diametrically opposed to that of the Christian worldview.

So, before we can enter into an honest and informed discussion of the social justice movement, we need to take a closer look at the foundation and infrastructure that God, our authority as followers of Christ, has established for society. We will then be better equipped to evaluate the claims of social justice advocates.

Nature's Foundation for Society

So we begin with the most basic of all questions: What is God's foundation for society? The simple answer is Himself. God is the foundation for everything. But taking this a bit further, because God is our authority, His Word and His law are our authorities as well. If God, His Word, and His law are ever rejected, there is no foundation for truth.

Thus, these three things—God's divine being, God's divine revelation, and God's divine law—are the foundation of society. And it's not coincidental that they also answer the most basic question of each of the three main branches of philosophy:

~ What is ultimate reality? (Ontology)

~ How do we know what we know? (Epistemology)

~ Who decides what is right and wrong? (Ethics)

Every worldview or philosophical system is rooted in the answers given to these three ultimate questions. Everything we believe (that is, if we are consistent in our thinking) can be traced back to at least one of these three questions. For this reason, our answers to them determine how we view and understand everything else about the world around us.

What Is Ultimate Reality?

Is there a God, an ultimate being, who created the universe, or is the universe all there is? Is something nonmaterial and nonphysical (like God, mind, or reason) ultimate, or is something material and physical ultimate? Can the universe explain itself without needing to presuppose the existence of a transcendental and personal God,

> **ontology**
>
> the branch of philosophy that deals with the nature of being and existence and the relationship between all existing things

or is a transcendental and personal God necessary to explain why there is something rather than nothing?

How Do We Know What Is Real and True?

Is there a God who communicates universal truth in nature, as the Bible claims (Psalm 19; Romans 1), or are we left to figure out all the answers for ourselves? Are we born with innate

> **epistemology**
>
> the branch of philosophy that deals with how knowledge is ascertained

knowledge of reality and truth? Or do we come into this world as a blank slate, lacking immediate awareness of God and His law? Does all knowledge begin with sense experience, as most atheists argue? Or, as the Bible claims, does all knowledge begin with the knowledge of God?

Who Has the Right to Decide What Is Right and Wrong?

If God as the creator of all things exists, and if He has communicated to us what is right and wrong, then who but God has the authority to tell us how to live our lives? If there is a God, then He has the right to define gender roles and delegated authority structures, such as the family. He has the right to define the purpose of man's existence. But if

> **ethics**
>
> the branch of philosophy that deals with the relationship between morality and behavior

there is no God, then who is to decide? The government? The individual? The rich and powerful? The mob? Or, as some claim, is there no way of knowing objectively what is right or wrong?

These Answers Are Interlocking

Just as His Word and His law cannot be disconnected from God Himself, the answers to these three foundational questions cannot be separated. How we answer any one of them determines how we will answer the other two. For instance, if a scientist says all knowledge comes from sense experience, then that scientist must conclude that a personal and transcendent God—if He exists at all—is entirely unknowable. And removing a personal and transcendent God from the realm of what is knowable would naturally lead to ethical relativism. Without a personal and transcendent God, there is no divine truth or divine law to provide us with any universal standard, and thus, what is morally right or wrong fluctuates from people group to people group, and even from individual to individual.

These Answers Are of Primary Importance

Consequently, the answers to these questions are of utmost importance. We can be wrong about many things, like who won the 1976 World Series, and still have a cohesive and reliable worldview. But if we get these fundamental questions wrong, then everything else we believe will fail to have a foundation to rest on. How we answer these three questions determines everything else we think and do.

Thankfully, we don't have to wonder about the answers. As Christians, we believe that God has clearly, irrefutably, and universally revealed them in nature.

Nature Provides Us with the Answers

Nature teaches us certain undeniable truths—truths so evidently displayed we don't need human instruction to understand them. For example, a child can discover that fire is hot and ice is cold experientially, and the truth of that teaching will override any human instruction to the contrary.

This applies to more than just the physical realities of our universe. The Bible makes it clear that the foundational truths for society are also clearly revealed in nature. Romans 1 and 2 and Psalm 19 inform us that every person throughout history, from the center of the largest city to the edge of the remotest island, is without excuse because God has universally, immediately, and undeniably—without the help of human instruction—revealed three certainties:

1. There is a God (Ps. 19:1–3).

2. We know there is a God (Rom. 1:20).

3. We know the difference between right and wrong (Rom. 2:12–16).

No matter where we look, we observe the imprint of God's creative design and power in the universe. We perceive that He is God—the ruler and maker of all things. In short, we see and know in our hearts that God is the ultimate authority.

We cannot help but see God's authority in His law, (which He has written in our consciences) and in His design (which He has stamped on the things He has made). And by observing God's design in His creative works, we cannot help but perceive their intended purpose. Looking at a pair of needle-nose pliers, for example, we can see why they were invented. In the same way, God made His purpose for each created thing clear by its very design. This is as evident when we consider the biological distinctions between men and women as it is when we consider the design distinctions between a monkey and a fish. Every created thing has meaning and purpose assigned by God and is immediately understood by observing God's intentional design in all things.

But does design necessarily communicate purpose? Absolutely. The design existed in the mind of the designer before it was embodied in the created thing, and the created thing was brought into existence to fulfill the specific purpose intended by the creator. Think again of needle-nose pliers. The inventor had a specific purpose for creating that design. Atheists, however, say meaning and purpose come after existence. Because there is no divine creator, there is no divine purpose to anything, they insist. That's like saying needle-nose pliers were created for no purpose, and only later was it discovered what they were good for. In the same way, atheists posit that the universe just happens to exist with no design and for no intended purpose. And because man just *is*, according to atheists, he gets to decide for himself his own existential purpose for life. Man is his own authority. So if a man decides he is in fact a woman, the atheist—or anyone else, for that matter—has no grounds to say otherwise.

But if God does exist, then man is not his own authority and does not get to decide his own meaning. Seeing design in nature reveals not only the Designer but also the Designer's purpose for all things. It is essential to acknowledge God's authority in His design because this is what gives us understanding of our purpose and is the basis of the authority for our worldview. In other words, because we know we are created in God's image for God's glory, we know that (1) we have the authority to obey God and (2) no one has the authority to tell us otherwise.

This, then, leads to the natural question that if God is indeed the authority to which man is responsible, how is that responsibility communicated from the Creator to those under authority? For communication to be effective, a point of connection or similarity must exist between the one transmitting and the one receiving the information. For humanity, this connection was established by God when He created man in His own rational and ethical likeness. And though this connection has been damaged in the fall, our thinking is still embedded with logical and moral distinctions that have no foundation outside of God. Such distinctions within our conscience allow us to know God and to know right from wrong. Therefore, though there is a Creator-creature distinction, there is a real point of similarity between God and us that allows us to know God by knowing ourselves.

It is this connection with God, though tainted by sin, that allows God to effectively communicate transcendental and universal truths to His image-bearers through the natural world He created for this very purpose. This is vital, for if there is no universal truth, then language—the tool in which we conceive divine truth in our minds—becomes nothing more than a cultural construct lacking any authority. By making us in His image, God has secured a way to effectively and authoritatively speak to us in both natural and special revelation.

Language is not always fluid and culturally constructed. Universal truths, such as the laws of logic and the knowledge of good and evil, transcend culture and are communicated in every language. God has clearly communicated to all people, no matter the language they speak, the foundation for all things: a divine Being, divine revelation, and a divine law. Without these core presuppositions, a worldview has no ultimate authority to rest on. The knowledge of God is essential to universal truth and universal morality, and universal truth and universal morality are essential to the credibility and consistency of any worldview. Without universal and objective truth, the self-refuting claim of relativism is all that remains. Without an ultimate authority, there is no basis for any authority.[1]

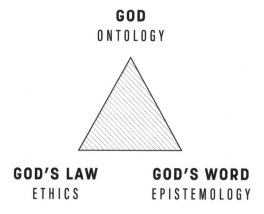

GOD
ONTOLOGY

GOD'S LAW   **GOD'S WORD**
ETHICS   EPISTEMOLOGY

---

1 See Jeffrey D. Johnson, *The Absurdity of Unbelief* (Conway, AR: Free Grace Press, 2016).

These three universal truths are designed by God to be the foundation of society. And these three core presuppositions can be reduced to a single concept: divine authority. Once this divine authority is abandoned by a society, that society is bound to be abandoned by God. History has proven time and again that if a society walks away from what it knows to be true, it will inevitably be drawn down the dark, well-worn path of self-destruction.

Nature's Infrastructure for Society

Social justice's war with divine authority not only attacks the foundation but also the infrastructure God has provided for society. And by "the infrastructure of society," I mean the basic building blocks of society, such as the individual, the family, the state, and the church.

How are individuals to relate to each other? What authority, rights, and freedoms do they have? What role does the family play in society? What makes up the family, and how is the family to be governed? What role does the state have in maintaining law and order? What is the separation of church and state? How much authority does the state have?

These are the basic questions we need to answer before we begin evaluating the claims of social justice. For we must bear in mind that social justice is a sociological ideology with its own precommitments. It may be that social justice is an ideology that doesn't accept the sanctity of human life, in which all our individual rights are rooted. It may be that this ideology doesn't accept the nuclear family as the backbone of society. It may be that this ideology doesn't accept the limited authority of the state in organizing and structuring society. It may be that social justice is at war with the God-given institutions of society.

So, before we evaluate social justice, it's key for us to establish the authority and the jurisdiction God has given to (1) the individual, (2) the family, (3) the state, and (4) the church.

The Individual

We begin with the individual, for the individual is the most basic building block of society. Society is made up of individuals. But what authority has God given to the individual? What are the rights and freedoms of the individual? In sociology, this is the most basic and important of all questions. Before we talk about how people are to interact with each other, is it not vital to determine what rights belong to each person and where those rights come from?

The Authority of the Individual

As Christians, we acknowledge that our rights and freedoms come from God. It is self-evident that our rights and freedoms are rooted in the sanctity of human life. Unless we are psychopathic, our own innate and irresistible desire to live a happy and meaningful life leads us to the inescapable conclusion that all life is priceless and precious. Just as it is self-evident we are to treat others as we want to be treated, it is obvious, through the recognition of the sanctity of our own lives, that we know all life is sacred.

The sanctity of human life comes from being designed in the likeness of God (Gen. 1:27). Unlike animals, we are designed to bring glory to God by personally knowing, enjoying, representing, and serving Him in all that we think and do. The amazing blessing of being made to serve God elevates our lives beyond self-interest and gives us a transcendental purpose and ethic for living.

But if we claim there is no God, we must then conclude that we have no ultimate meaning, purpose, value, or ethic. Without God, we are just animals. People often want to live for self and as if there were no God, but they fail to realize that without God,

nihilism

the philosophical notion that everything, including human life, is meaningless.

the meaninglessness of nihilism is all that remains. Thus, to deny God's existence is to deny the sanctity and true value of our own lives.

So it is clear that being made in the image of God gives us meaning. This not only provides us with a transcendental purpose but also a universal ethic. And because all humans are made in the image of God, we are called to protect human life from the womb to the tomb and to treat everyone as we would like others to treat us.

The sanctity of human life also grants each of God's image-bearers other inalienable rights:

- ~ the right to life
- ~ the right to protect life
- ~ the right to work and provide for one's life
- ~ the right to marry and raise a family
- ~ the right to worship God according to conscience

In other words, the sanctity of human life is the foundation and authority of our inalienable rights. These God-given rights—as well as the right to protect and safeguard them—are founded in the reality of being made in God's image.

We were designed to represent God by working and taking dominion (Gen. 1:26, 28; 3:19). Because this is a responsibility from God, it's a right and a freedom. We are entitled to work and provide for ourselves. In fact, God's Word takes this even further and teaches us we reap what we sow (Gal. 6:7), a worker is worthy of his wages (1 Tim. 5:18), and that if we don't work, we don't eat (2 Thess. 3:10).

We also have the authority to protect our God-given rights from all those who may attempt to take them from us. No one—be it a spouse or parent, a religious institution or church, or even a civil authority—has the right to infringe upon these inalienable rights given to us directly by God.

Moreover, because of the sanctity of human life, we are all responsible to acknowledge, protect, and defend these rights not only for ourselves but for each other. Thus, the basic authority (rights and freedoms) of the individual is the first delegated institution of power under God.

The Jurisdiction of the Individual

It should go without saying, then, that no one has the right to sin against God or to violate the rights of other individuals. Our freedom extends only to the authority and jurisdiction that has been given to us image-bearers. We have freedom as long as we submit to God's law, the standard for true justice. This is a basic truth of nature.

The Patriarchal Family

Though God made man as an individual before He instituted marriage, He didn't design man to live alone (Gen. 2:18). Men and women are made to be codependent (1 Cor. 11:11). This is another basic truth revealed by God in nature. Man and woman were designed for each other. God has implanted natural attraction between men and women and provided the marriage union to satisfy and safeguard these natural desires.

The Authority of the Family

Thus, in the natural order of things, the second realm of delegated jurisdiction is the authority of marriage, where two become one flesh. Together, the husband and wife have the authority to take dominion, have sexual intimacy, have and raise children, and protect the individual rights of each family member.

Marriage was designed with a patriarchal head who leads a submissive wife for the purpose of taking dominion and propagating and raising the next generation of individuals. All these objectives are fleshed out in the early chapters of Genesis. Nature tells us, as

> **patriarchy**
>
> the system in which husbands are the leaders of the family and called to take principal roles of leading, providing, and protecting women and children

does common sense, that the family consists of a man and a woman joined together by God, under the leadership of the husband, for the purpose of taking dominion through hard work and raising and nurturing children in the fear of the Lord.

God has imbued the family with the authority and responsibility to protect the inalienable rights of the individuals within the family. God has given the family, principally the husband, the responsibility to provide for its individual members and to protect them from all enemies and forces—including overreaching civil authorities—that would attempt to encroach on their freedom to obey God.

The family, as God has designed it, is the backbone of society. How is the next generation to be properly raised up to maturity? How will society function without responsible, disciplined, educated citizens? It is the family that God designed to raise up, discipline, and educate the proceeding generations of individuals.

But for this process to function properly, the family itself must function properly. First, God has designed men to be masculine; it is imbedded in their biological nature. Far from being "toxic," masculinity is vital for society. True masculinity allows a man to be strong and brave so he can protect and lead his wife and children and, if necessary, go to war and fight to safeguard the freedoms God has given all of us.

Next, God has designed women to be feminine. True femininity gives a wife the strength to be gentle in caring for her husband and patient in the nurturing of her children. Within the framework of a family, nature reveals the gender roles that distinguish men and women from each other.[2] In other words, the difference between masculinity and femininity is not a social construct but something built into the biological nature of men and women. And finally, God has instructed children to be in submission to their parents to learn discipline and self-control. So we see that if any of these parts are compromised, the family breaks down, with the destruction of society following soon afterward.

The Jurisdiction of the Family

It is essential to note that man was made as an individual before he was made to be given in marriage—the marriage union does not nullify the individual's God-given rights and responsibilities. We have the authority to guard and protect our inalienable rights whether in a state of singleness or a state of monogamy.

Marriage does not cancel the individual rights of husbands, wives, or children. We all must obey our consciences, for we all must personally give an

---

2 For an excellent resource on the distinct roles of men and women, see Owen Strachan and Gavin Peacock, *The Grand Design: Male and Female He Made Them* (Ross-shire, UK: Christian Focus, 2016).

account to God for how we lived our lives. Though a wife is to submit to her husband, she has the right to defend herself from an abusive husband. Likewise, children are under no obligation to subjugate themselves to abusive parents.

Civil Authorities

Individuals and families are not made for government; government is made for individuals and families. Civil authority is the third realm of delegated authority by God. This institution is necessary because sin entered the world. Because of lawlessness and injustice, God provided a third institution of authority—the state—to punish lawbreakers and protect the innocent.

The Authority of Civil Authorities

It is imperative to realize that civil authorities do not bestow individuals and families their rights and freedoms. It is the state's responsibility, as it rules under God, to protect the freedoms and rights of individuals and the family. Consequently, civil authorities have been given the power of the sword—the judicial and legal power to punish evildoers to keep the peace (Rom. 13:4; 1 Tim. 2:2).

Because civil authorities have been sanctioned by God to protect us from malefactors, we are called to obey our civil leaders and pay our taxes:

Let every person be subject to the governing authorities. For there is no authority except from God, and those that exist have been instituted by God. Therefore whoever resists the authorities resists what God has appointed, and those who resist will incur judgment. For rulers are not a terror to good conduct, but to bad. Would you have no fear of the one who is in authority? Then do what is good, and you will receive his approval, for he is God's servant for your good. But if you do wrong, be afraid, for he does not bear the sword in vain. For he is the servant of God, an avenger who carries out God's wrath on the wrongdoer. Therefore one must be in subjection, not only to avoid God's wrath but also for the sake of conscience. For because of this you also pay taxes, for the authorities are ministers of God, attending to this very thing. Pay to all what is owed to them: taxes to whom taxes are owed, revenue to whom revenue is owed, respect to whom respect is owed, honor to whom honor is owed. (Rom. 13:1–7)

The Jurisdiction of Civil Authorities

Though the state is separate from the church, the state is not separate from God. All institutions of power have authority only as they operate under the authority of God by upholding justice. God has bestowed on the individual and the family certain rights, and no civil authority has the right to infringe upon those rights.

The Church

The freedom for individuals to worship God according to their conscience is revealed in nature. Nature allows for the freedom of religion. The state and church must remain separate from each other; otherwise, religious persecution is bound to occur.

The Authority of the Church

The authority of the state is natural revelation, and the authority of the Christian church is special revelation—the Scriptures. The church's doctrine, worship, discipline, practices, and mission come from the Bible—and the Bible alone. The church is separate from the state, with a distinct jurisdiction, because the church derives its authority directly from God and not from the state. This ensures that the church's authority is not undermined by outside powers, doctrines, philosophies, or influences. It is vital that the church submits to God to maintain its authority; otherwise, the sufficiency and authority of Scripture will be compromised.

This means that the church has the authority to not only preach the Bible but also to assemble in worship and send missionaries into every nation. The church does not need to get permission from any civil authority to do what God has called it to do.

The Jurisdiction of the Church

For the state to interfere with the church or for the church to surrender its authority to the state would be a failure of the church in its submission to God, who is the head of both the church and the state.

Separate Branches of Delegated Authority

These four institutions of power—the individual, the family, the civil authority (the state), and the church—do not receive their authority from each other but directly from God.

In addition, each of these delegated authorities have their own sphere of jurisdiction that is not to be infringed upon by the other institutions. The church does not answer to the state any more than the state answers to the church. Neither the church nor the state has the right to take the education of children away from the family. A family cannot declare war on another nation, nor does a husband have the right to rule over the conscience of his wife. And the state can never forbid a church from assembling.

Each of the separate institutions of delegated power will give a direct account to God for how they exercised their limited authority over their God-given and restricted jurisdictions. To keep tyranny at bay, it is crucial for each institution of power to stay confined to its God-prescribed jurisdiction.

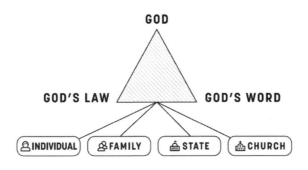

This division of power is a protection against the abuse of power. For example, the state is to intervene when parents overstep their authority by violating the rights of the children, as in the case of abuse. However, the state should not interfere in family matters when the family is operating in a just manner. It's wise that the state does not oversee the affairs of the church nor the church manage the dealings of the state. No institution of authority has the right to abuse their power by restricting the rights and freedoms of the other branches of authority.

Only God is all-powerful, and God will not share that status with anyone. Knowing that man's heart is evil, we should consider it a blessing that His delegated power has been divided among separate jurisdictions. For, as they say, absolute power corrupts absolutely. Thus, when these distinct jurisdictions remain separate, society will function as God has intended.

For this reason, every institution of power is under God's moral law. Law and order and justice and equity are to guide society and keep peace among individuals, families, and nations. In sum, without God's law as revealed in nature, justice and peace cannot exist in society.

But God's divine authority, which underpins the Christian worldview and any stable society, is fundamentally rejected by and diametrically opposed to the worldview that lies at the heart of social justice. The worldview of social justice is rooted in atheism, relativism, and the denial of a universal standard of right and wrong. And it began with Karl Marx.

2

THE FOUNDATION OF SOCIAL JUSTICE

If we are going to jump on the social justice band-wagon and join those who chant for justice and equality for women, blacks, minorities, homosexuals, and anyone else who is not a white male, it would do us well to know what they mean by justice and equality. It might be that these words mean something different for them than they do for Christians. Perhaps we have two different dictionaries. It may be that the worldview that shapes how they define, and thus understand, the meaning of things is determined by a different authority than the one underpinning the Christian worldview—God.

To get a grasp of what social justice advocates mean by *justice* and *equality*, we need to understand their worldview. We need to examine what lies underneath the painted walls of justice and equality and take a look at the foundation and infrastructure of their beliefs.

In this chapter we will inspect the *foundation* of social justice—classical Marxism. In the following chapter, we will take a look at the *infrastructure* of social justice—critical theory. And, in chapter 4, we will be forced to conclude that social justice is a new morality at war with true justice.

The origins of social justice, at least as it is currently defined, can be directly traced back to Karl Marx (1818-1883). The Marxist roots of this movement are not something social justice advocates are hiding—they are rather proud of this. For instance, Patrisse Cullors, co-founder of Black Lives Matter (BLM), identifies herself and her fellow organizers of BLM as "trained Marxists."[1]

Karl Marx was born in Germany in 1818. After studying in Paris, he moved to London in 1852—the great city where the "Prince of Preachers," Charles Spurgeon (1834-1892), was preaching the gospel. While Marx lived in London, Spurgeon would become the most renowned minister of his day.

---

1   "A Short History of Black Lives Matter," The Real News Network, July 23, 2015, YouTube, https://youtu.be/kCghDx5qN4s.

Whereas there is no indication that the two men ever met face-to-face, the famous preacher increasingly warned his hearers of the dangers of Marxism. In response, as author David Aikman recounts, Marx's *Communist Manifesto* cowriter, Friedrich Engels, referred to Spurgeon as the person he hated most in the world.[2] This was the beginning of the battle of worldviews that continues to rage in our nation and in our pulpits today.

The Foundation of Marxism

It was for good reason that Spurgeon and Marx opposed each other—their beliefs stood on conflicting and opposing foundations. To take a closer look at the basis of Marx's ideology, we must understand that Marx rejected what Spurgeon believed was the foundation for all knowledge—God.

The Ontology of Classical Marxism

You see, Marx was an avid atheist; he rejected the idea of God. And not just that, Marx sought to construct a new philosophical worldview consistent with his atheism. Like Friedrich Nietzsche (1844–1900), who would arrive on the scene a few years later, Marx was willing to throw out everything connected to God in order to reconstruct a new philosophy of life.

---

2 David Aikman, *The Delusion of Disbelief* (Carol Stream, IL: Salt River, 2008), 106–107.

While some atheists only want to get rid of God while keeping all authority of the individual and family that flow from God, Marx wanted to purge everything associated with God. The radical he was, Marx was willing to go all the way with his denunciation of theism. He was prepared to rethink everything, including the family, from the ground up and start afresh.

Marx was eager to eliminate everything associated with God so he could rebuild a new system of beliefs founded on the fluid and ever-shifting foundation of atheism. Thus, the old stone foundation had to go, along with the infrastructure that stood upon it. Everything built on theism had to be removed, every stone uprooted and cast into the abyss, so that everything could be reconstructed from scratch.

And this is what Marx sought to do in the construction of his communistic worldview. He made this clear in *The Communist Manifesto* (1848) when he and co-author Friedrich Engels (1820–1895) declared, "Communism abolishes eternal truths." Everything truth-related to God and eternity must be thrown out. Communism begins on a totally new foundation. As Marx and Engels went on to say, "It abolishes all religion, and all morality, instead of constituting them on a new basis."[3]

---

3 Karl Marx and Frederick Engels, *The Communist Manifesto* (New York: International Publishers, 2020), 22.

With no transcendental God and no eternal truths to light the way, what was this new foundation on which Marx chose to construct his philosophy? According to Marx, the material universe is all that exists, which means that physical matter, not God, is the ultimate reality. Mind, soul, emotions, mathematics, logic, knowledge, ethics, and everything else that is immaterial must be rooted and derived back to the material universe. In sum, the ontological foundation for communism is materialism.

> **materialism**
>
> the philosophical precommitment that all things can be reduced to physical matter

The Epistemology of Classical Marxism

Therefore, for Marx, we only have the light of the material cosmos to guide us. There is no point in looking for any outside help. Why there is something rather than nothing must have a self-explanation. And if we are forced, due to a precommitment to atheism, to only look from within the cosmos for answers, we must conclude that science—the study of material objects—is our only valid source for knowledge.

> **empiricism**
>
> the theory that all knowledge begins and is restricted to that which can be ascertained by sense experience

Of course, Charles Darwin (1809–1882) provided a materialistic and "scientific" theory for the origins of life, which Marx would wholeheartedly embrace in 1859. Regardless of whether evolution is a valid explanation of how life originated from lifeless matter, it is the only materialistic theory of cosmology that doesn't look outside the cosmos for the answer.

Consequently, being consistent with his atheistic ontology, Marx was a committed empiricist in his epistemology. That is to say, according to Marx, all knowledge begins with and is limited to sense experience. Nothing outside our empirical senses can guide us because nothing transcends the empirical universe. And nothing transcends this empirical universe because our senses do not sense any transcendent being—so the circular reasoning goes.

> **tabula rasa**
>
> the theory that individuals are born without any built-in mental content

Like the materialistic empiricists who went before him, such as John Locke and David Hume, Marx believed that infants are born completely innocent and ignorant. On this blank slate of innocence and ignorance is written only that which is taught by society and ascertained by one's experiential senses. And the only way to verify what is taught by society is by looking to science.

The idea that science is the only reliable way of authenticating truth is known as positivism. Positivism claims that every justifiable assertion must either be self-verifying or verified by scientific evidence, by logical proof. The famous example of a self-verified statement is "All bachelors are single." This is true because singleness is what it means to be a bachelor. Such a statement is true because of the impossibility of the contrary. No self-verifying ideas must, therefore, be substantiated by science.

> **positivism**
>
> the notion that science is the foundation of all knowledge

William Clifford (1845–1879), a British mathematician and philosopher, argued for positivism when he claimed, "It is wrong always, everywhere, and for anyone, to believe anything upon insufficient evidence."[4] Another famous atheist, Bertrand Russell (1872–1970), likewise claimed, "Whatever knowledge is attainable must be attained by scientific methods; and what science cannot discover, mankind cannot know."[5]

Consequently, positivism rules out God because the statement "God exists" is neither self-verifying nor able to be verified by science.

---

4 W. K. Clifford, "The Ethics of Belief," in *Philosophy of Religion*, ed. Charles Taliaferro and Paul J. Griffiths (Oxford: Blackwell, 2003), 199.

5 Bertrand Russell, *Religion and Science* (Oxford: Oxford University Press, 1997), 227.

It doesn't appear, however, that Clifford and Russell realized that positivism is self-refuting. In short, positivism doesn't meet its own demands. The statement that "all non-self-verifying statements must be verified by science" is neither a self-verifying statement nor is it attested by any scientific evidence. Science does not prove that all truth is confined to the empirical senses—for such a statement transcends the reach of the empirical senses. How can science, therefore, know if matter is all that exists?

Science can explain some things, but it can't explain everything. Science can't even explain itself. This is evident in the fact that science can't justify the existence of the immaterial laws of nature which science itself can't operate without.

Thus, I am not sure how Marx, Clifford, and Russell knew that all knowledge is limited to scientific knowledge. But regardless of the glaring inconsistency of positivism, Karl Marx was committed to positivism in the formation of his atheistic worldview.

The Ethic of Classical Marxism

The ethics taught by Spurgeon were derived from natural and special revelation. According to Spurgeon, the book of nature and the book of Scripture both teach that we are to love God with all our hearts and to love our neighbors as ourselves. This provides the world with a universal and objective ethic.

But because Marx rejected Spurgeon's God, he also rejected Spurgeon's ethic. Just as Marx was forced to root his epistemology in his materialism, he was forced to root his ethic in materialism. Of course, this led him to reject any notion of sin, which is a transgression against God, or any inherited depravity, which is a selfish disposition enslaved to sin. With the rejection of such ideas, Marx believed that man is born as an innocent materialistic machine or animal waiting to be programmed by the culture. Many years later, Bertrand Russell echoed this claim:

> **sin**
>
> the transgression of God's law

> Materialists used the laws of physics to show, or attempt to show, that the movements of human bodies are mechanically determined, and that consequently everything that we say and every change of position that we effect fall outside the sphere of any possible free will. If this be so, whatever may be left for our unfettered volitions is of little value. If, when a man writes a poem or commits a murder, the bodily movements involved in his act result solely from physical causes, it would seem absurd to put a statue to him in the one case and to hang him in the other case.[6]

---

6 Russell, 37–38.

According to Russell, these misbehaved machines do not need to be shamed or punished; they need to be fixed and treated medically:

> No man treats a motorcar as foolishly as he treats another human being. When the car will not go, he does not attribute its annoying behavior to sin; he does not say, "You are a wicked motorcar, and I shall not give you any more petrol until you go." He attempts to find out what is wrong and to set it right. An analogous way of treating human beings is, however, considered to be contrary to the truths of our holy religion.[7]

This, of course, removes all culpability and responsibility from bad behavior and criminal acts. As Russell went on to explain,

> It is evident that a man with a propensity to crime must be stopped, but so must a man who has hydrophobia and wants to bite people, although nobody considers him morally responsible. A man who is suffering from a plague has to be imprisoned until he is cured, although nobody thinks him wicked. The same thing should be done with a man who suffers from a propensity to commit forgery; but there should be no more idea of guilt in the one case than in the other.[8]

Since sinful behavior is the result of a malfunction of body, the cure is not in holding the criminals

---

7 Russell, 40.
8 Russell, 41.

accountable but in treating their physical bodies with physical medication. Their problem is a "chemical imbalance" of the brain. They, as Russell said, don't need to be blamed or punished but pitied. They need to be treated as mentally sick, not as criminals. They are not morally responsible but victims of thinking and behavior they cannot help.

Nevertheless, though Russell was only eleven years old when Marx died, Marx would have agreed with Russell. According to Marx, the ills of society are the result of some materialistic and physical illness—not because of the depraved and selfish dispositions within humanity. Man's behavior is conditioned by the chemicals in the brain as well as *external* social and historical factors. Man's own moral problems, if they are not reducible to a mental illness, are the result of poor parenting, poor education, and poorly organized societies. Don't blame the criminal; blame his parents or society. Criminals are just the victims of a dysfunctional society.

Thus, to fix man's behavior issues and the ills of society, Marx reasoned, we must fix these external institutions of power. The problem is not within man, as James declares

determinism

the philosophical notion that all events are determined completely by the laws of nature that were set in place at the beginning of the cosmos

(James 4:1), but within the institutions of society. In other words, for Marx, the problems vexing society have nothing to do with mankind being in a hostile relationship with God. They are, rather, the fault of institutions of society. The problem, as they say, is *institutional* or *systemic*.

Another dreadful consequence of ethics being rooted in materialism is *determinism*. If the laws of science are what determine behavior, then not only is man not morally responsible for his actions but he also has no free will. As with all other cosmic events, every action that takes place in the universe has been set in order at the beginning of the big bang. Unlike divine providence, with a sovereign God working alongside secondary causes and free moral agents to carry out a master plan, determinism is everything being mindlessly and purposelessly predetermined without a master plan. It is dreadful because it is *blind* fatalism.

However, Marx was not a pessimist. He was a Hegelian. Heavily influenced by dialectics of Georg Wilhelm Friedrich Hegel (1770–1831), Marx was convinced that society was slowly, naturally progressing away from capitalism to communism. Like evolution in animals, the deterministic laws of science were naturally pushing society from chaos to utopia. Of course, communism should be encouraged and hurried along by the working class, but Marx believed a global classless state is the inevitable conclusion of history. It was just a matter of time, in Marx's mind, before communism took over the world.

In sum, the three-pillar foundation for Marx's worldview comprises materialism, positivism, and determinism.

MATERIALISM
ONTOLOGY

DETERMINISM   **POSITIVISM**
ETHICS   EPISTEMOLOGY

The Infrastructure of Marxism

On this three-prong foundation, Marx intellectually built the infrastructure he believed was consistent with his atheistic worldview. As we shall see, none of the institutions established by God—individual, family, church, and state—will remain standing because, according to Marx, society can be divided between the Haves and the Have Nots. The Have Nots don't have as much as the Haves because they have been unjustly oppressed by the Haves. The Haves have more because of a rigged, unfair, and unjust system. For Marx concludes, "Hitherto, every form of society has been based, as we have already seen, on the antagonism of oppressing and oppressed classes."[9] Consequently, "the history of all hitherto existing society is the history of class struggles. Freeman and slave, . . . lord and serf, guild-master and journeyman, in a word, oppressor and oppressed."[10]

To work for another and be under the authority of a boss or a supervisor is to be enslaved and oppressed, Marx claimed. There is no justification for business owners to make more money than the working class who do the work. Not only are business owners oppressing their workers, but the whole capitalistic infrastructure that allows for such free enterprise and entrepreneurship is inherently oppressive and unjust. As long as a discrepancy of wages and wealth exists, there is injustice in the system. Marx explained the injustice of capitalism this way: "Not only are they slaves of the bourgeois class, and of the bourgeois state; they are daily and hourly enslaved by the machine, by the overlooker, and, above all, by the individual bourgeois manufacturer himself."[11]

For the Have Nots to have less than the Haves is the ultimate act of injustice. It is simply not fair, they say, that some people have a bigger piece of the

---

9 Marx and Engels, *The Communist Manifesto*, 14.
10 Marx and Engels, 9.
11 Marx and Engels, 10.

pie, more of this world, than others. And, thus, for Marx, the great problem to be overcome in society is the *unjust and unequal distribution of power and wealth.* This is the materialistic ethic of Karl Marx—eliminate "evil" by replacing capitalism with communism. The Have Nots will not be free until all people work for themselves and are under the authority of no one but the collective voice of the universal class. Not until a classless society (with no hierarchal chain of authority) of economic equality is created will the world be free of injustices and inequalities.

Marx believed that the great moral problem of society could be reduced to the institutions of authority within society. He held that because authority by its very nature is oppressive, all authoritative structures and institutions must be destroyed. And when all decentralized divisions of authority have been dismantled, a globalized classless society must take its place in a new world order. In this new world order, people will no longer have to relate to each other as superiors and inferiors, rich and poor, leader and follower. Not until there are no class divisions, diversity, or hierarchical stature of authority will society be free of oppression. Only then will the world be rid of evil and experience utopia.

Thus, on the godless foundation of atheism, Karl Marx drew up a plan of redemption to rebuild a new infrastructure based on communism. But first, before construction can begin, there needs to be total demolition of the current infrastructure of society. Before resurrection of the new, there must be death to the old. The current institutions of society must fall before communism can rise out of the ashes.

But most importantly, because our present institutions derive their delegated authority from God, these institutions (individualism, family, church, and state) must first be deconstructed and stripped of their authority in order to fully eliminate God from society. In fact, for Marx, deliverance from the evils of capitalism cannot occur until all traces of God are removed from this world.

The Deconstruction of the Inalienable Rights of Individuals

The current infrastructure of society, at least as designed by God, begins with the individual rights and freedoms that God has personally and directly given to each of His image-bearers. As pointed out in the previous chapter, each inalienable right is rooted in the sanctity of human life, and the sanctity of human life is rooted in the reality that every person is made in the image of God. In other words, God holds everything together.

On this foundation God laid the infrastructure of the various institutions of society—individual authority, family authority, state authority, and church authority. And this starts with each individual having the right and authority to protect their own life and the lives of others, the right to marry and raise a family, the right to work and provide materialistically for themselves and their family, and the right to worship God according to their own personal conscience.

This is a crucial part of the delegated authority God has given his image-bearers that no other delegated institutional authority (family, church, and state) has the right to take away. Yet, because Marx rejected God, God cannot be the source of man's individual authority, rights, and freedoms.

According to Marx, it is not God or the laws of nature that give man his rights and freedom. He believed that just because nature teaches us that we reap what we sow, it doesn't make it just for some to reap more than others. It is not fair for some to be rich and others to be poor. The reason some individuals have more wealth than others is not necessarily because some work harder or take more risk than others but because the current system allows the rich to get richer at the expense of the working class.

Where wealth has been accumulated, Marx argued, it has been accumulated through an unjust system—capitalism. The freedom that allows individuals to start their own businesses and accumulate personal property and wealth must be taken away for the sake of fairness and equality. Wealth must also be taken from the rich and redistributed to the masses. *The Communist Manifesto* made this very clear: "The theory of the Communists may be summed up in the single sentence: Abolition of private property."[12] It seems by this logic that only when no one owns anything will there be fair and equal distribution of wealth for everyone.

For this to happen, a radical revolution must take place by the working class. They must act. As *The Communist Manifesto* cries out, "The immediate aim of the Communists is the same as that of all other proletarian [working class] parties: formation of the proletariat [masses] into a class, overthrow of the bourgeois supremacy, conquest of political power by the proletariat."[13]

The Deconstruction of the Family

But the deconstruction of individual freedom is not enough. Marx believed the family must be destroyed as well. Let me be as clear as I can, Christians and churches who are entertaining social justice are courting a movement that has no room for God, individual freedom, or the family, as this founding father of social justice made clear when he taught that in the same way private businesses oppress their workers, the traditional family oppresses women and children.

12 Marx and Engels, *The Communist Manifesto*, 23.
13 Marx and Engels, 22.

The authority of God, the individual, and the family must all be dismantled. In fact, all delegated institutions of power are to be consolidated into one centralized, global power that evenly distributes wealth to a classless society. *The Communist Manifesto* made this objective clear:

> Abolition of the family! Even the most radical flare up at this infamous proposal of the Communists. On what foundation is the present family, the bourgeois family, based? On capital, on private gain. In its completely developed form, this family exists only among the bourgeoisie. But this state of things finds its complement in the practical absence of the family among the proletarians, and in public prostitution. The bourgeois family will vanish as a matter of course when its complement vanishes, and both will vanish with the vanishing of capital. Do you charge us with wanting to stop the exploitation of children by their parents? To this crime we plead guilty. But, you say, we destroy the most hallowed of relations, when we replace home education by social.[14]

Marx's co-author and friend, Friedrich Engels, in his book *The Principles of Communism,* asks the question, "What will be the influence of communist society on the family?" He goes on to answer by declaring that it will be the end of the traditional nuclear family:

14 Marx and Engels, 26–27.

It will transform the relations between the sexes into a purely private matter which concerns only the persons involved and into which society has no occasion to intervene. It can do this since it does away with private property and educates children on a communal basis, and in this way removes the two bases of traditional marriage—the dependence rooted in private property, of the women on the man, and of the children on the parents.[15]

This, of course, is an attack on the very fabric of society. God designed the nuclear family—the very backbone of society—to train, discipline, and nurture the next generation of leaders and workers. Remove the authority structure of the family, and society is only one generation away from its own demise.

But this is what Marx believed needed to happen for communism to be fully implemented and functional. He believed the hierarchical authority and oppression of the husband and the authority and oppression of parents would continue to be propagated from one generation to the next as long as the nuclear family was in charge of educating their own children.

> **hierarchy**
>
> the chain of command descending from greater authority to lessor authorities

Consequently, communism required not only that the family be broken apart but that responsibility for

---

15 Friedrich Engels, *The Principles of Communism* (N.P.: Pattern Books, 2020), 37.

education be stripped from the family and centralized under the direction and authority of the state:

> And your education! Is not that also social, and determined by the social conditions under which you educate, by the intervention direct or indirect, of society, by means of schools, &c.? The Communists have not invented the intervention of society in education; they do but seek to alter the character of that intervention, and to rescue education from the influence of the ruling class.[16]

In other words, children do not belong to their oppressive parents; they belong to the people. It is the village's responsibility to indoctrinate the next generation of workers.

The Deconstruction of Civil Authorities

God has wisely decentralized earthly powers into separate institutions for a good reason. Absolute authority belongs only to God. The decentralization of power is a natural check and balance to the abuse of power. For their own safety, God separated the nations at Babel for this very reason.

But this, too, Marx believed needed to be reversed. Communism will only function properly, he reasoned, as a global initiative. This new world order can have no borders, no distinct national sovereignty, and no classification of people. Likewise, Engels asks the

---

16 Marx and Engels, *The Communist Manifesto*, 27.

question, "Will it be possible for this revolution to take place in one country alone?" and then proceeds to answer:

> No. By creating the world market, big indus-
> try has already brought all the peoples of the
> Earth, and especially the civilized peoples, into
> such close relation with one another that none
> is independent of what happens to the others.
> Further, it has coordinated the social develop-
> ment of the civilized countries to such an extent
> that, in all of them, bourgeoisie and proletar-
> iat have become the decisive classes, and the
> struggle between them the great struggle of the
> day. It follows that the communist revolution
> will not merely be a national phenomenon but
> must take place simultaneously in all civilized
> countries.[17]

The Reconstruction of Communism

According to *The Communist Manifesto*, it will take time to deconstruct the institutions of society and rebuild a classless society. The Communist revolution of the people will not take place overnight. But to help move things forward, Marx and Engels provided some measured steps of action:

1. Abolition of property in land and application of all rents of land to public purposes.

2. A heavy progressive or graduated income tax.

---

17   Friedrich Engels, *The Principles of Communism*, 31 (Question 19).

3. Abolition of all rights of inheritance.

4. Confiscation of the property of all emigrants and rebels.

5. Centralisation of credit in the hands of the state, by means of a national bank with State capital and an exclusive monopoly.

6. Centralisation of the means of communication and transport in the hands of the State.

7. Extension of factories and instruments of production owned by the State; the bringing into cultivation of waste-lands, and the improvement of the soil generally in accordance with a common plan.

8. Equal liability of all to work. Establishment of industrial armies, especially for agriculture.

9. Combination of agriculture with manufacturing industries; gradual abolition of all the distinction between town and country by a more equable distribution of the populace over the country.

10. Free education for all children in public schools. Abolition of children's factory labour in its present form. Combination of education with industrial production.[18]

And Engels, in question 16 in his book *The Principles of Communism,* claimed,

18 Marx and Engels, *The Communist Manifesto,* 30–31.

It would be desirable if this could happen, and the communists would certainly be the last to oppose it. Communists know only too well that all conspiracies are not only useless, but even harmful. They know all too well that revolutions are not made intentionally and arbitrarily, but that, everywhere and always, they have been the necessary consequence of conditions which were wholly independent of the will and direction of individual parties and entire classes. But they also see that the development of the proletariat in nearly all civilized countries has been violently suppressed, and that in this way the opponents of communism have been working toward a revolution with all their strength. If the oppressed proletariat is finally driven to revolution, then we communists will defend the interests of the proletarians with deeds as we now defend them with words.[19]

In question 17, Engels went on to ask, "Will it be possible for private property to be abolished at one stroke?" He answered his own question by saying,

No, no more than existing forces of production can at one stroke be multiplied to the extent necessary for the creation of a communal society. In all probability, the proletarian revolution will transform existing society gradually and will be able to abolish private property only when the means of production are available in sufficient quantity.[20]

---

19 Engels, *The Principles of Communism*, 25 (Question 16).
20 Engels, 25.

Then in the answer to question 18, "What will be the course of this revolution?" Engels provided these steps of action:

1. Limitation of private property through progressive taxation, heavy inheritance taxes, abolition of inheritance through collateral lines.

2. Gradual expropriation of landowners, industrialists, railroad magnates and shipowners, partly through competition by state industry, partly directly through compensation in the form of bonds.

3. Confiscation of the possessions of all emigrants and rebels against the majority of the people.

4. Organization of labor or employment of proletarians on publicly owned land, in factories and workshops, with competition among the workers being abolished and with the factory owners, in so far as they still exist, being obliged to pay the same high wages as those paid by the state.

5. An equal obligation on all members of society to work until such time as private property has been completely abolished.

6. Centralization of money and credit in the hands of the state through a national bank with state

capital, and the suppression of all private banks and bankers.

7. Increase in the number of national factories, workshops, railroads, ships.

8. Education of all children, from the moment they can leave their mother's care, in national establishments at national cost. Education and production together.

9. Construction, on public lands, of great palaces as communal dwellings for associated groups of citizens engaged in both industry and agriculture and combining in their way of life the advantages of urban and rural conditions while avoiding the one-sidedness and drawbacks of each.

10. Destruction of all unhealthy and jerry-built dwellings in urban districts.

11. Equal inheritance rights for children born in and out of wedlock.

12. Concentration of all means of transportation in the hands of the nation.[21]

---

21 Engels, 27–28.

Sounding the Alarm

Charles Spurgeon saw the peril of Marxism and was not afraid to speak against it. In June of 1878, while preaching on Psalm 118, he warned of its dangers, as well as those, especially within the church, who advocate for socialism:

> German rationalism which has ripened into Socialism may yet pollute the mass of mankind and lead them to overturn the foundations of society. Then "advanced principles" will hold carnival and free thought [i.e., atheism] will riot with the vice and blood which were years ago the insignia of "the age of reason." I say not that it will be so, but I should not wonder if it came to pass, for deadly principles are abroad and certain ministers are spreading them.[22]

Spurgeon knew that Marxism not only seeks to destroy the foundation of society but also undermines personal sin and the gospel of Jesus Christ in the process. In April 1889, while preaching on Isaiah 66, Spurgeon proclaimed,

> For many a year, by the grand old truths of the gospel, sinners were converted, and saints were edified, and the world was made to know that there is a God in Israel. But these are too anti-

---

[22] Larry Alex Taunton, "Karl Marx vs Charles Spurgeon: An Epic Struggle for the Souls of Men in 19th-Century London," published July 29, 2020, https://larryalextaunton.com/2020/07/karl-marx-vs-charles-spurgeon-an-epic-struggle-for-the-souls-of-men-in-19th-century-london.

quated for the present cultured race of superior beings! They are going to regenerate the world by Democratic Socialism, and set up a kingdom for Christ without the new birth or the pardon of sin. [23]

I, too, want to join Spurgeon in blowing the trumpet and warning of the dangers of social justice. To think social justice is just about ending unjust oppression, racism, sexism, and gender inequality is to be unaware that it is rooted in Marxism—which has no room for God, individual freedom, the nuclear family, the church, or any form of nationalism.

---

23 Taunton, "Karl Marx vs Charles Spurgeon."

3

THE EVOLUTION OF SOCIAL JUSTICE

If the house of social justice is built on the foundation of classical Marxism, then the framing is constructed from critical theory. If we look below the surfaces of the "sexual revolution," the feminist and gay rights' movements, and the Black Lives Matter organization, we will discover the common infrastructure of critical theory.

The Origins of Critical Theory

Critical theory sprung from classical Marxism. Many committed Marxists in the 1920s had become disillusioned with classical Marxism. Marxists in Germany and Austria were increasingly concerned that communism was not taking root in the European nations. Though Marxism was implemented in the Soviet Union in 1922, it was being rejected elsewhere. Moreover, they knew that for Marxism to flourish and spread, it had to be accepted and welcomed by the masses around the world. It must be a global revolution of the people for the people. But where was the uprise? Where was the frustration against capitalism? Where were the demands for a new world order—a rebuilt society of justice and equity?

In his Hegelian determinism, Marx believed communism would naturally overtake capitalism around the world. Sooner or later, the progressive evolutionary process of the laws of economics was bound to create a global classless society. Yet, in the 1920s, it still seemed that the majority of the Have Nots remained content working for the Haves. It appeared that wives remained happy to live under the leadership of their husbands. And it looked as if nationalism was alive and well.

> **critical theory**
>
> a social philosophy of class warfare that claims language is social construction used as a means of oppression by those in power and calls for the deconstruction of power structures through the deconstruction of language

According to the disillusioned Marxists, some new tactic was needed to awaken the masses from their slumber. Marx was under the impression that communism would naturally spread on its own. But the disciples of Marx were beginning to think otherwise. More radical measures needed to be taken to motivate the Have Nots to take action.

Before there would be democratic global socialism, the majority of those who are oppressed and under the authority of another (be that a husband, parent, or boss) must be stirred into such a frenzy of discontentment and frustration that they collectively push all established institutions of authority down. Only then can a classless and global society of equality and justice with no hierarchical structures of authority arise.

Georg Lukács and Karl Korsch

The first two Marxists to question classical Marxism were Georg Lukács (1885–1971) and Karl Korsch (1886–1961). Georg Lukács was an active member of the Hungarian Marxist Party who sought to make a slight revision to classical Marxism. He highlighted his concern in his book *History and Class Consciousness*, published in 1923. Likewise, his friend Karl Korsch, a member of the German Marxist Party, published his *Marxism and Philosophy* in 1923, outlining his issues with Marxism.

Their concern was rooted in the epistemology of classical Marxism. Marx was committed, as we have seen, to positivism. Lukács and Korsch were not so convinced that the findings of science were able to be interpreted without being misread by one's cultural biases. These cultural biases are often so subtle they remain hidden in the interpreter's unconsciousness. Lukács, for example, argued, "There is no objective reality which social theorists can passively reflect upon; for at every moment they are part of the societal process as well as its potential critical self-awareness."[1]

Lukács eventually moved to Moscow and found work at the Marx-Engels Institute. Korsch fled Germany in 1936 for the United States and taught at Tulane University in New Orleans before moving to New York to work at the International Institute for Social Research.

The Frankfurt School

Lukács' and Korsch's slight move away from classical Marxism helped set in motion the rise of the Frankfurt School and what is now known as Western Marxism, better known today as social Marxism.

The Frankfurt School, or more technically known as the Institute for Social Research, at the University

---

1 Quoted in David Held, *Introduction to Critical Theory: Horkheimer to Habermas* (Berkeley, CA: University of California Press, 1980), 21.

of Frankfurt, Germany, was founded in 1923 by Marxist law professor Carl Grünberg (1861–1940), the first avowed Marxist to hold a chair at a German university, and was funded, ironically, by a wealthy merchant, Felix Weil (1898–1975). Though Weil was born into wealth, he was a committed Marxist who wrote his doctoral dissertation on the practical problems of implementing Marxism. This is fitting, because the Frankfurt School, the first Marxist research center in Germany, was dedicated to one thing—researching how best to implement Marxism around the world.

The Frankfort School was committed to teaching and implementing Marxist ideas into every division of education—philosophy, sociology, history, law, and psychology. It gathered a team of Marxist professors to do just that. Some of the more notable scholars were Theodor Adorno (1903–1969), Walter Benjamin (1892–1940), Erich Fromm (1900–1980), and Max Horkheimer (1895–1973), who would take over leading the program in 1930.

And it was Max Horkheimer who first coined and defined critical theory in his 1937 essay, *Traditional and Critical Theory*.

The Foundations of Critical Theory

The foundation for critical theory is social Marxism. Building off the work of Lukács and Korsch, the Frankfurt School rejected one of the threefold foundational pillars of classical Marxism, positivism, and replaced it with relativism.

The Ontology of Critical Theory—Materialism

Like classical Marxism, social Marxism is founded on atheism. This did not change. Social Marxism is just as godless as classical Marxism, if not more so.

The Epistemology of Critical Theory—Relativism

The Frankfurt School became more consistent with their atheism by rejecting positivism and embracing relativism. The universal laws of science have God's fingerprint stamped on them. Like God, they are authoritative and binding—regardless of how one may "feel" about them. As one of the leading proponents for social justice today, Robin DiAngelo, said, "Critical theory developed in part as a response to this presumed superiority and infallibility of scientific method, and raised questions about whose rationality and whose presumed objectivity underlies scientific methods."[2]

---

2 Özlem Sensoy and Robin DiAngelo, *Is Everyone Really Equal?: An Introduction to Key Concepts in Social Justice Education* (New York: Teachers College Press, 2012), 4.

And the famed social Marxist and community activist Saul Alinsky (1909–1972) claims, "Men have always yearned for and sought direction by setting up religions, inventing political philosophies, creating scientific systems like Newton's, or formulating ideologies of various kinds. This is what is behind the common cliché, 'getting it all together'—despite the realization that all values and factors are relative, fluid, and changing, and that it will be possible to 'get it all together' only relatively."[3]

Marx may have flirted with relativism with his obsession with the materialistic dialectics of Hegel, but the Frankfurt School all out embraced it. They were even willing to throw out the laws of nature. According to Horkheimer, even the laws of nature cannot be comprehended outside of one's subjective experiences, which have been encoded in one's thinking by one's cultural context.

The Frankfurt School also believed that not only were the history books written by those in power at the time but that the meaning of language was determined by those in power as well, making language itself a tool used by the powerful to maintain their power.

Because reality can only be understood through the ever-changing prism of one's cultural context,

3 Saul D. Alinsky, *Rules for Radicals: A Practical Primer for Realistic Radicals* (New York: Random House, 1972), xv. See also pp. 10, 11.

one's cultural context is the principal oppressor—especially if it has been shaped in any way by theism. Thus, the greatest danger of oppression, according to social Marxists, is the oppression that imprisons people's thinking without them even knowing it. Those who believe in God and in traditional values, for instance, are the most oppressed by the cultural institutions because they are informed by the history and language of the ruling class and willingly submit to the norms of an oppressive society.

The Ethics of Critical Theory—Anti-Authority

But like classical Marxists, social Marxists are committed to communism as the solution to the institutional and systemic oppression that permeates society. They, too, rejected any notion of depravity and sin against a holy God. They did not place the ills of society within man's depraved heart but, rather, within the external institutions of society, such as the traditional family.

The Frankfurt School was heavily influenced by Sigmund Freud (1856–1939). The Institute's sociology and psychology departments integrated Freudianism with their Marxist ideology.

Essentially, Freud claimed that behavior was influenced by three levels of consciousness:

1. the id—the unconscious mind, which includes one's basic desires and impulses

2. the ego—the conscious mind, which is shaped by society

3. the superego—the ego seeking to suppress the id, one's basic desires, and bring them into conformity to social norms

Thus, the id, which Marx believed was the "true you," is conflicted by one's ego (i.e., conscience), which has been shaped by the cultural constructs of society. This internal conflict of the mind (i.e., the superego) is what brings frustration and oppression to one's thinking. It is what brings guilt. For instance, the young teenager who is struggling with homosexual desires may feel guilty because his conscience has been unjustly shaped by his religious upbringing. Such guilt keeps him oppressed and prevents him from being who he wants to be. It keeps him from expressing his "true identity."

Freud reasoned that this internal war brings a false sense of shame, confusion, and frustration. Therefore, the cure to man's internal conflict and false guilt is found only in the dismantling of the cultural constructs that bring about the false sense of guilt. The external norms that suppress the id from coming out of the closet must be removed. Not until all social norms of the past are dismantled will the id be fully free to express itself without conflict or shame.

The Frankfurt School held that morality, then—especially conservative values—was socially constructed to keep the inward desires of the powerless and oppressed class from being free to express themselves. This oppression will continue as long as these values are maintained by the old institutions of power, such as the family.

MATERIALISM
ONTOLOGY

ANTI-AUTHORITY
ETHICS

RELATIVISM
EPISTEMOLOGY

The Infrastructure of Critical Theory

On the threefold foundation of social Marxism— atheism, relativism, and anti-authority—critical theory emerged. The word *critical* comes from the critical approach the Frankfurt School took to the knowability of reality and truth. They believed that knowledge is confined to language and that language has been socially constructed by the subjective and ever-changing contextual "values" of those in power.

Without man being made in God's image, which allows effective and authoritative divine communication, this makes sense. In other words, with no divine revelation, there can be no universal truth. And without universal truth, language has no foundation for its own meaning.

Thus, for the Frankfurt School, language is a social construct of the ruling class used as a means of oppression. And therefore, language is oppressive. French philosopher Jacques Derrida (1930–2004) carried forth these ideas in three books all published in 1967: *Of Grammatology, Writing and Difference,* and *Voice and Phenomenon.* Because knowledge is the construction of language, and because language is the construction of socially constructed definitions written by those in power, knowledge becomes a means of power and oppression. Michel Foucault (1926–1984), for instance, coined the term *power knowledge* in 1981, claiming that "knowledge is a construct of power." For Foucault, rather than truth being objective, it operates as "regimes of truth." "Each society," Foucault claimed, "has its regime of truth, its 'general politics' of truth: that is, the types of discourse which it accepts and makes function as true; the mechanisms and instances which enable one to distinguish true and false statements, the means by which each is sanctioned; the techniques and procedures accorded value."[4]

Psychoanalyst Wilhelm Reich (1897–1957), who took over Sigmund Freud's outpatient clinic and wrote *The Sexual Revolution* in 1936, claimed, "Marx found social life to be governed by the conditions of economic production and by the class conflict that resulted from these conditions at a definite point of history. It is only seldom that brute force is resorted to in the domination of the oppressed classes by the owners of the social means of production; its main weapon is its ideological power over the oppressed, for it is this ideology that is the mainstay of the state apparatus."[5]

It's not necessarily jails or prisons that keep the Have Nots oppressed; it is language itself that is holding them down. The Haves define the meaning of words, and such proscribed meaning is what keeps the Have Nots in line and submissive. And this is the heart of critical theory—any authoritative meaning that passes itself as objective truth is inherently discriminating and oppressive.

Therefore, critical theory seeks to deconstruct

---

4 Paul Rabinow, ed., *The Foucault Reader* (New York: Pantheon, 1984), 73.
5 Wilhelm Reich, "Social Function of Sexual Oppression," in *German Essays on Psychology*, Wolfgang Schirmacher and Sven Nebelung, eds. (New York: Continuum, 2001), 153.

objective meaning wherever it's found. Critical theory is applied to the study of law (critical legal theory), the study of history (critical history theory), the study of sexuality and gender (critical gay theory and critical gender theory), and the study of race (critical race theory).

But in all this, the objective is to deconstruct meaning, which they deem is intolerant, to liberate the so-called oppressed from the unjust bondage of those who are in power—or as the director of the Frankfurt School, Max Horkheimer, said, "to liberate human beings from the circumstances that enslave them."[6] For Horkheimer, the endgame of such liberation is "individual self-emancipation and self-creation."[7] In other words, to have liberation (from God), all authority and meaning and traces of God must be deconstructed because authority is inherently oppressive in their worldview.

The objective of the Frankfurt School was to study the best way of implementing the liberation of Marxism, and they concluded it would not happen without reeducation. But before you can teach people the value of Marxism, you must inform them of the dangers of capitalism. People who are happy with the way things are must become disillusioned with

---

6 Max Horkheimer, *Critical Theory* (New York: Seabury, 1982), 244.
7 See David Held, *Introduction to Critical Theory*, 25.

the way things are. They are unknowingly oppressed and, thus, need to be informed of their oppression. They need to be *awakened*. If ever they are going to collectively break out of the social prison that enslaves them, they must become discontent with the "Establishment."

The Frankfort School scholars knew this type of revolution would not happen overnight. Horkheimer recognized it would take time, for famously he claimed, "The Revolution won't happen with guns, rather it will happen incrementally, year by year, generation by generation. We will gradually infiltrate their educational institutions and their political offices, transforming them slowly into Marxist entities as we move towards universal egalitarianism."

Long ago they determined to use the universities as their churches to reindoctrinate the masses and convert new followers to their pursuit of justice and equality. From the universities they would train up community leaders and politicians, continuing this process generation after generation until they controlled the mainstream media and outlets of communication. And without guns or bombs, the populace would be convinced that something radically needed to happen to the current Establishment.

Before the Establishment as a whole can be overthrown, however, the various institutions of society must be overthrown (the authority of the individual, the family, and civil governments). As David Held explains, "The purpose of theory . . . is to analyze and expose the hiatus between the actual and the possible, between the existing order of contradictions and a potential future state. Theory must be oriented, in short, to the development of consciousness and the promotion of active political involvement."[8]

The Deconstruction of the Family

But rather than attempting to undermine the authority of the individual and one's inalienable rights first, this would come last in the process. First, the authority of the patriarchal family needed to be assaulted by

> **patriarchy**
>
> the system in which husbands are the leaders of the family and called to take principal roles of leading, providing, and protecting women and children

the radical left. The traditional values of complementarianism, gender roles, sexuality, and parenting needed be deconstructed. The traditional family is restricting and oppressive, even to those who willingly embrace it.

This assault on the traditional family started many years ago with the sexual revolution and the feminist movement in the 1960s and has continued with the

---

8   David Held, *Introduction to Critical Theory: Horkheimer to Habermas* (Oxford, UK: Polity, 2004), 22.

gay, bisexual, and transgender movements of our own day. This decay can be chronicled by observing how the family is represented in TV sitcoms over the last sixty years.

David Held, in his book *Introduction to Critical Theory*, explains why the Frankfurt School was so adamant about the necessity of deconstructing the family: "The family is the mediator between the economic structure of the order and its ideological superstructure."[9] Horkheimer states,

> The family has a very special place among the relationships which through conscious and unconscious mechanisms influence the psychic character of the vast majority of men. . . . The family, as one of the most important formative agencies, sees to it that the kind of human character emerges which social life requires, and gives this human being in great measure the indispensable adaptability for a specific authority-oriented conduct on which the existence of the bourgeois order largely depends.[10]

The family, in his view, is the building block of the dangerous infrastructure of authoritarianism.

As Held further explains,

> The birth of Capitalism emancipated the family

---

9 Held, *Introduction to Critical Theory*, 126.
10 Max Horkheimer, *Authority and the Family*, accessed February 6, 2021, https://cominsitu.files.wordpress.com/2019/01/max-horkheimer-authority-and-the-family.pdf, 98.

from serfdom. Yet the family retained a pseudo-feudal, hierarchical structure as the direct personal dependence of women and children survived in the home. The power of the father was always based on the dependence of others; he had the capacity to give or withhold things that were greatly wanted. Under Capitalism the basis of his authority was, at least for a period, reinforced; 'father' rules the roost not only in virtue of his physical strength but also because he is often the sole breadwinner. The relative isolation of women and helplessness of children in the home strengthens his position.[11]

Moreover, Horkheimer claimed that the family perpetuates generational authoritarianism:

[The son] may think what he will of his father, but if he is to avoid conflicts and costly refusals he must submit to his father and satisfy him. The father is . . . always right where his son is concerned. The father represents power and success, and the only way the son can preserve in his own mind a harmony between effective action and the ideal, a harmony often shattered in the years before puberty's end, is to endow his father, the strong and powerful one, with all the other qualities the son considers estimable. . . . Childhood in a limited family becomes an habituation to an authority which in an obscure way unites a necessary social function with power over men.[12]

And as if that were not enough, Horkheimer

---

11 Held, *Introduction to Critical Theory*, 129.
12 Horkheimer, *Authority and the Family*, 107–108.

asserted the authoritarianism of the family is at the heart of man's psychological problems: "The lack of independence, the deep sense of inferiority that afflicts most men, the centering of their whole psychic life around the ideas of order and subordination, but also their cultural achievements are all conditioned by the relations of child to parents or their substitutes and to brothers and sisters.[13]

Likewise, psychologist Erich Fromm, another member of the Frankfurt School, agreed: "The instinctual apparatus itself is a biological given; but it is highly modifiable. The role of primary formative factors goes to the economic conditions. The family is the essential medium through which the economic situation exerts its . . . influence on the individual's psyche."[14]

Wilhelm Reich, the author of *The Sexual Revolution* and *Social Function of Sexual Oppression*, claimed that only "under non-capitalist and non-patriarchal institutions people could live honestly, industriously and co-operatively."[15] And according to David Held, "Reich's conclusions as to what could bring about an end of this state of affairs included recommendations establishing the sexual rights of all—including

---

13   Horkheimer, 108–109.
14   Rainer Funk, "Erich Fromm's Concept of Social Character," *Social Thought & Research* 21, no. 1/2 (1998): 215–29, accessed February 8, 2021, http://www.jstor.org/stable/23250038.
15   Quoted in Held, *Introduction to Critical Theory*, 116.

children and adolescents."[16]

It is the authoritarian patriarchal father who suppresses the sexual desires of children, keeping the next generation enslaved in an out-of-date morality. Reich claimed, "We do not conceal the fact that we want to protect children and adolescents from being inculcated with sexual anxiety and guilt feeling." Thus, for Reich, sexual health can be defined as the "freedom from any kind of ascetic moralizing attitudes."[17]

For this reason, critical theory is not only committed to destroying the traditional family but also to removing education out of the home and into the public square. Instruction of the next generation needs to be the responsibility of the state to ensure oppression does not continue to forthcoming generations. For, as Hillary Clinton famously stated, "It takes a village."

Finally, critical theory demands that parental rights be slowly removed and children be able to make more and more decisions on their own without parental consent. Eventually, any parent who objects to their child undergoing a sex change or an abortion will be seen as abusers who need to be arrested.

---

16 Held, 117.
17 Wilhelm Reich, *The Sexual Revolution*, trans. Therese Pol. (New York: Farrar, Straus and Giroux, 1974), 279.

The Deconstruction of Civil Authority

The goal of Marxism has always been global in intent. All classes and demographical divisions must be eliminated. Marx made this clear in his day, and the social Marxism of the Frankfurt School was not any different. The decentralization of power is a safeguard against the abuse of power, but such decentralization, according to critical theory, only incites authoritarianism of one nation over the others. This can be seen, they say, in the colonization of lands belonging to native people groups around the world by the industrial nations of Europe.

For the Frankfurt School, nationalism, like racism, is an oppressive idolatry of superiority. Nations such as America, they would say, were built on oppression. According to this way of thinking, America was formed on the confiscation of lands that belonged to the Native Americans and then was built up on the backs of slaves. That's why the tagline "Make America Great Again" is deemed as offensive and racist—in the eyes of some, America has never been great.

Furthermore, nationalism must fall before there can be an open and borderless society. More and more power must be relocated from the state to the national level and then from the national level to the international level. The way for governments to relinquish their national sovereignty is by turning the focus to global concerns and dangers, such as climate change, that are best confronted by a global economic effort.

The Deconstruction of Individualism

Finally, the authority and inalienable rights and freedoms of the individual must be taken away and consolidated into one globalized power of "equality." The right to life and self-protection, the right to take dominion and gather personal property, and the right to free speech and to worship God according to conscience all must be removed for Marxism to work.

Free speech is dangerous because words are dangerous. Language is how the traditional values of oppression and authoritarianism spread. Such oppression must be removed for people to feel free to "sin" without a guilty conscience.

And the freedom to take dominion and gather personal wealth and property also must be seized from the individual. Too much personal property and wealth is oppressive as it supposedly limits and hinders others from their fair share. If some have more than they need, this means that others will have less than they need.

Though individual freedom may seem to be the hardest of the God-given institutions to deconstruct, the far left has been doing a good job at getting people to willingly give over their rights to the state. You see, there is more than one way to take away individual freedom—by force, by fear, or by exchange.

Personal freedoms can be taken away by brute force, but this hypothetically goes against critical theory's ideologies of anti-oppression and authoritarianism. They would rather take away individual freedom by fear. This is how political correctness works. Make people feel so ashamed to use certain words that they willingly give up the freedom of speech. Get people so scared of a spread of a pandemic that they willingly submit to being micromanaged by big government. Create fear and offer safety, and people will give you almost anything you ask them.

But it seems the most effective way of confiscating personal freedoms is by exchanging them for free handouts. Freedoms come from God, and no government or power has the right to take them away. Yet the state can confuse people as to what their rights are. So, because critical theory advocates do not believe in God, they don't believe human rights come from God. And by claiming that free healthcare and free cell phones and free college tuition and free money are human rights (which only big government can give to everyone), they can help get people to willfully exchange their God-given freedoms for a hot bowl of porridge.

4

THE INJUSTICE OF SOCIAL JUSTICE

If critical theory is social Marxism applied, social justice is critical theory applied. And because critical theory is at war with all forms of authority, social justice is the rallying cry for activists to take down all institutions of authority.

However, it is important to understand the difference between true *justice* as defined in Webster's dictionary and the "justice" envisioned by the social justice movement. Social justice is not concerned about the fair and impartial treatment of all people or the just punishment of lawbreakers. But that is the goal of true justice—law and order—and this is what must guide our society for it to remain standing. True justice is based on the universal law of God that demands fair treatment and righteous judgment and exacts consequences on those who violate the law.

Social justice, by its very nature, is not just. It wants to remove any objective standard, labeling the moral law of God a social construct designed by white men to keep their subjects obedient. Their understanding of justice is at war with true justice. According to Scott David Allen, social justice is about "the tearing down of traditional structures and systems deemed to be oppressive, and the redistribution of power and resources from oppressors to victims in pursuit of equality of outcome."[1]

In other words, the objective of social justice is not making sure every basketball player gets to play by the same set of rules and is treated equally—this is the old standard of justice. The objective of social justice is to make sure every player has equal playing time and equal points and that no team loses the game. With no losers, everyone gets a participation trophy. The more athletic and skilled the player, the harsher the player must be treated to make things fair for the less athletic and skilled players. This understanding of justice has nothing to do with law and order and everything to do with equal outcome, equal wages, and equal distribution.

---

1 Scott David Allen, *Why Social Justice Is Not Biblical Justice* (Grand Rapids: Credo House Publishers, 2020), 43.

For social justice to work, so its advocates think, true justice must fail since it is based on a binding and authoritative law and thus is inherently oppressive. It binds the present generation with an antiquated construct of a previous generation—a generation that defined what was right and wrong intentionally to keep the Have Nots in line and under their thumb. As Saul Alinsky boldly uttered, "Justice, morality, law, and order are mere words when used by the Haves, which justify and secure their status quo."[2]

Therefore, in the minds of Marxists, the only way for there to be social justice is for true justice to be destroyed. The tall players must be cut down a size or two to make it fair for the shorter guys. One must steal from those who are born with "advantages" to give to those who are at a supposed disadvantage. But Moses warned against perverting true justice: "You shall not pervert justice. You shall not show partiality, and you shall not accept a bribe, for a bribe blinds the eyes of the wise and subverts the cause of the righteous. Justice, and only justice, you shall follow" (Deut. 16:19–20).

The Have Nots can be subdivided into many classes of oppression and poverty: women, minorities, immigrants, blacks, and gays—even left-handed people—as well as those who are transgender,

---

2 Saul D. Alinsky, *Rules for Radicals: A Practical Primer for Realistic Radicals* (New York: Random House, 1972), 19.

handicapped, obese, and short. The more categories of oppression a person identifies or intersects with, the more disadvantages and oppression they face. These flaws are embedded in our society, making it systemically and institutionally oppressive, sexist, racist, homophobic, transphobic, and unjust.

> **intersectionality**
>
> the idea, developed by Kimberlé Crenshaw, that some individuals, such as black women, are members of multiple oppressed groups who experience multiple layers of oppression, such as racism and sexism

Social justice advocates Sensoy and DiAngelo, in their book *Is Everyone Really Equal?*, explain it in this way: "A critical approach to social justice refers to specific theoretical perspectives that recognize that society is stratified (i.e., divided and unequal) in significant and far-reaching ways along social group lines that include race, class, gender, sexuality, and ability. Critical social justice recognizes inequality as deeply embedded in the fabric of society (i.e., as structural), and actively seeks to change it.[3]

The Foundation of Social Justice

The core tenet of social justice is the same as that of critical theory: language is oppressive. And

---

3 Özlem Sensoy and Robin DiAngelo, *Is Everyone Really Equal? An Introduction to Key Concepts in Social Justice Education* (New York: Teachers College Press, 2012), xviii.

language is oppressive because language is inherently value-laden.

For instance, concerning the relativism of social Marxism, Sensoy and DiAngelo claim—the irony of relativists proclaiming to know something with objective certainty aside—that "we know that knowledge evolves over time and is dependent on the moment in history and the cultural reference point of the society that accepts it."[4]

And concerning the idea that language and knowledge is oppressive, Robin DiAngelo claims,

> Understanding knowledge as socially con-structed uncovers the role of ideology in the construction of history: for example, the idea that progress is the result of a rational, objec-tive, and value-neutral process, one that is removed from any political agenda; a prod-uct of reason alone. This picture of progress supports the belief that there is an objective truth, that it belongs to the West, and that this truth can be applied universally. This notion of objectivity was central to rationalizing the col-onization and exploitation of other lands and peoples that began in the 15th century."[5]

DiAngelo goes on to say,

> One of the key contributions of critical theo-rists concerns the production of knowledge.

---

4 Sensoy and DiAngelo, 2.
5 Sensoy and DiAngelo, 3.

Given that the transmission of knowledge is an integral activity in schools, critical scholars in the field of education have been especially concerned with how knowledge is produced. These scholars argue that a key element of social injustice involves the claim that particular knowledge is objective and universal. An approach based on critical theory calls into question the idea that "objectivity" is desirable, or even possible. The term used to describe this way of thinking about knowledge is that knowledge is socially constructed. When we refer to knowledge as socially constructed we mean that knowledge is reflective of the values and interests of those who produce it."[6]

In a way of illustrating how language is oppressive, DiAngelo goes on to explain:

Consider the first question most people ask expectant parents, "Is it a boy or a girl?" Why do we ask this question? We ask this question because the answer sets in motion a series of expectations and actions. For example, if parents are informed that they are having a girl, they may begin to buy clothes and decorate the room in preparation for their daughter's arrival. The colors they choose, the toys they buy, their expectations for her future will all be informed by what that culture deems appropriate for girls. But even our conception of what girls and boys are is rooted in our culture. Although sex and gender are often used interchangeably, they mean different things.

6 Sensoy and DiAngelo, 7.

> Sex refers to the biological, genetic, or pheno-typical characteristics that are used to distin-guish female and male bodies: genitals, body structure, hormones, and so on. These biolog-ical differences among humans are necessary for reproduction. Gender, on the other hand, is what it means to have that body in that cul-ture. Gender refers to the roles, behaviors, and expectations our culture assigns to those bodily differences: how you are "supposed" to feel and act based on whether your body is seen as female or male. Males are expected to learn to "act like a man"—they are trained into "mas-culinity"; and females are expected to learn to "act like a woman"—they are trained into "femininity."[7]

This understanding of how language works is at the heart of social justice. To transition from the old-world order, which is based on divine, delegated, and authoritative institutions, into a new world order of centralized power of a classless society, the longstanding ideas, ideologies, and concepts of intolerance must die out completely. To thoroughly rid society of God, all associations to objective and authoritative meaning must be expelled. So, because God's signature is stamped on every aspect of His creation—including language—everything in His created order must be deconstructed. For atheists to live without restraint and guilt, everything related to God must be deemed as oppressive and unjust.

---

7 Sensoy and DiAngelo, 15–17.

Since language is the principal means of conveying values, concrete meaning, and truth, it's the principal means of oppression. To get rid of oppression, the subjective opinion of the interpreter must override the objective meaning of the author. Such objectivity must, therefore, be exposed as oppressive and then afterward deconstructed of all its authority. Words either need to become fluid and flexible and nonthreatening or be so demonized as offensive that people are too ashamed to use them. In short, the ideas of white European men that shaped the values of Western civilization must be rejected and replaced.

The Infrastructure of Social Justice

Like Marxism, critical theory is at war with all hegemonic institutions of power, such as the individual, the family, civil authority, and the church. According to social justice, such distinct centers of power are the primary source of oppression and inequality. Thus, these institutions either have to go or be radically stripped of their power for true change to occur.

hegemony

the notion, developed by Italian communist Antonio Gramsci, of a dominant group imposing its own socially constructed values and knowledge onto marginalized groups in order to maintain power over them

The white, Western men of the Frankfurt School had a multigenerational plan to implement Marxism globally through the universities and education centers. Take over the school, and Marxist community leaders and politicians will eventually follow. Social justice is the fruit of that. Social justice is now an everyday conversation. It has thoroughly infiltrated the news, politics, entertainment, sports, social media, and even, sadly, many churches.

Social justice has grabbed a massive foothold in our society by focusing on race relations. By appealing to real injustices in our history regarding slavery and the Jim Crow laws, social justice activists were able to exploit the fact that most Americans and professing Christians repudiate such evils and do not want to be labeled "racists." They have done a masterful job of making people believe that social justice is the continuation of the political rights movement, led by Martin Luther King Jr., rather than the application of communism as conceived by Karl Marx.

But let me be clear. Social justice and critical race theory (CRT) and the gay rights movement are not the continuations of the political rights movement. Martin Luther King Jr. was seeking just laws. He was striving for fair treatment of all people, no matter one's ethnicity. He was seeking to confront true racism—treating others with prejudice and bias based on the color of their skin. This is evil, and God condemns such partiality (1 Tim. 5:21).

Social justice, as it changes the meaning of justice, has corrupted the meaning of the word *racism* to such an extent that it is now the justification of reverse racism against whites—especially against white males in positions of power.

How have social justice promoters been so successful in changing the meaning of justice and racism and getting so many people—even confessing Christians—to buy into these new definitions? The answer: by a constant barrage of gaslighting.

The term *gaslighting* originates from the 1938 play *Gas Light*, in which a husband tricks his wife into believing she has a mental illness by gradually dimming their gas-powered lights and telling her she is hallucinating. Gaslighting is a manipulation tactic, an attempt to slowly make someone question their own thoughts, perception, or judgment. And "in politics, the word 'gaslighting' is increasingly used to describe the left's efforts to push a false view of reality and to convince mainstream Americans that their common-sense views are somehow extreme."[8]

> **gaslighting**
>
> a manipulation tactic, an attempt to slowly make someone question their own thoughts, perception, or judgment

---

8   Timothy Daughtry, "Gaslighting and the Left's War on Reality," Townhall, January 4, 2017, https://townhall.com/columnists/timothydaughtry/2017/01/04/gaslighting-and-the-lefts-war-on-reality-n2267154.

With Marxist ideology already simmering in the universities, in 1971 social Marxist Saul Alinsky turned up the heat with his book *Rules for Radicals.* Because he embraced the relativism of his Marxist commitment, he was unashamed in casting off any moral or ethical restraints in the pursuit of power. Since he viewed the redistribution of power as a just cause, he believed such a noble end justifies whatever means. "In war," Alinsky declares, "the end justifies almost any means." Even committing crimes or rigging an election is justifiable, to Alinsky, if such lawless actions bring about the end of oppression because "the most unethical of all means is the nonuse of any means."[9]

And with the relativistic "the end justifies the means" ethic, there are five basic steps to tearing down the "unjust" authoritarian institutions of oppression and building a classless society:

1. Divide and conquer

2. Demonize institutions of power

3. Control the narrative

4. Relentlessly assault resisters

5. Make globalism the solution

Divide and Conquer

The first step in tearing down the hierarchical power

---

9 Alinsky, *Rules for Radicals,* 29; 26.

structures of society is to set people against each other. Divide people and then get them to turn on each other, as outlined by Alinsky:

> The disruption of the present organization is the first step toward community organization. . . . Fan the latent hostilities of many of the people to the point of overt expression. . . . Search out controversy and issues, rather than avoid them. . . . There can be no such thing as a "non-controversial" issue. When there is agreement there is no issue; issues only arise when there is disagreement or controversy. An organizer must stir up dissatisfaction and discontent; provide a channel into which the people can angrily pour their frustrations. He must create a mechanism that can drain off the underlying guilt for having accepted the previous situation for so long a time.[10]

Rather than allowing people to identify as Americans, which would bring some measure of unity, it is vital for the social justice champion to stimulate class warfare to bring people to the point where they hate America.

Race relations do not need to improve either, because this only aids in masking the current systemic oppression, injustices, and inequalities. If blacks cease to feel subjugated, they will cease to fight for revolution. If race relations are not continually

---

10 Alinsky, 117.

stirred up, there will be no protests or marches or riots demanding change. Progress cannot happen without a sense of rage.

And with greater hostilities, minorities should be encouraged to be loyal to their groups. Any independent thinking that deviates from groupthink must be viewed as a total betrayal to one's gender or ethnicity. For instance, according to Joe Biden, if you didn't vote for him, "then you ain't black."[11] But if you are like Candance Owens, a black woman who supported Donald Trump, you've betrayed your people and your voice is to be completely discounted.

This type of groupthink and identity politics is meant to pressure women and minorities not to break ranks. Until a classless society can be created, class warfare must continue. Such disunity will help people see the need for change, as Alinsky states, "A revolutionary organizer must shake up the prevailing patterns of their lives—agitate, create disenchantment and discontent with the current values, to produce, if not passion for change, at least a passive, affirmative, non-challenging climate."[12]

The benefit of this, according to Alinsky, is that you don't necessarily need a majority for the revolution to happen. All you need is for a very aggressive minority

---

11 Washington Free Beacon, "Biden: If You Don't Vote for Me, 'You Ain't Black'," YouTube, May 22, 2020, https://youtu.be/uBQ4PAT1hTg.

12 Alinsky, *Rules for Radicals*, xxii.

and a passive and silent populace that is willing to let the revolution occur without resistance. "Any revolutionary change," states Alinsky, "must be preceded by a passive, affirmative, non-challenging attitude toward change among the mass of our people. They must feel so frustrated, so defeated, so lost, so futureless in the prevailing system that they are willing to let go of the past and chance the future."[13]

In sum, the first step of deconstructing society is stimulating class warfare. This leads to their second step—blame the division on all the institutions that stand in the way of communism.

Demonize Institutions of Power

To rebuild Rome, you first must burn it down, and second, you need to blame it on the Christians. Once you have stirred up enough division, the second step is to turn people's frustration and hatred against the cultural constructs and authoritarian institutions that supposedly brought about all the oppression and inequality of wealth and power.

But the key to the second step is to take the focus off individual injustice by placing it on the evils of institutional power. Individual criminals on the street must be seen as the victims, and their lawless behavior as merely the natural result of the broken institutional systems in which they live.

---

13 Alinsky, xix.

As we saw in chapter 2, Marxists do not believe that the ills of society originate from within the depraved hearts of people, as the Bible claims, but from the external authoritative infrastructure of society. It's not personal prejudice that leads sinners to sin but the racist, sexist, and homophobic infrastructure of Western society organized and controlled by white men. As Robin DiAngelo claims,

> Oppression involves institutional control, ideological domination, and the imposition of the dominant group's culture on the minoritized group. No individual member of the dominant group has to do anything specific to oppress a member of the minoritized group; the prejudice and discrimination is built into the society as a whole and becomes normalized and taken for granted.[14]

According to DiAngelo, institutions are not only systemically oppressive but they also function together to keep the power and wealth in the hands of white men:

> Government is only one institution that men dominate. Men also dominate all other major institutions of society (military, medicine, media, criminal justice, policing, finance, industry, higher education, religion, and science). These institutions are interconnected

---

14 Özlem Sensoy and Robin DiAngelo, *Is Everyone Really Equal? An Introduction to Key Concepts in Social Justice Education* (New York: Teachers College Press, 2012), 39.

and function together to uphold male dominance across the whole of society.[15]

But that's not all. DiAngelo went as far as to
say, "If tomorrow only women were appointed to
government, they could not govern outside the
rules that men had established. To reshape the
institution and its norms and practices would take
generations of effort." In other words, under the
current infrastructure, there is no removal of racism,
sexism, or any other oppression. Even if all white
men handed over their positions of power and gave
their wealth to the poor and paid retributions to the
oppressed, oppression would still exist because the
oppressive infrastructure still exists. DiAngelo goes
on to conclude, "The reality is that no one can avoid
prejudices because it is built into our socialization."[16]

This is why there is no forgiveness for the sin of
racism in critical race theory (CRT). Every year a new
public statement of remorse and condemnation of
the sins of our nation and our institution must be
made. It is continual remorse without forgiveness
because the supposed racism will continue as long as
the institutions of power, like the family, exist.

This is also why, CRT devotees allege, if you are
white you can't help but be a racist. The UCLA School
of Public Affairs, in their affirmation of CRT, states:

---

15 Sensoy and DiAngelo, 45.
16 Sensoy and DiAngelo, 45; 31.

CRT recognizes that racism is engrained in the fabric and system of the American society. The individual racist need not exist to note that institutional racism is pervasive in the dominant culture. This is the analytical lens that CRT uses in examining existing power structures. CRT identifies that these power structures are based on white privilege and white supremacy, which perpetuates the marginalization of people of color. CRT also rejects the traditions of liberalism and meritocracy. Legal discourse says that the law is neutral and colorblind, however, CRT challenges this legal "truth" by examining liberalism and meritocracy as a vehicle for self-interest, power, and privilege. CRT also recognizes that liberalism and meritocracy are often stories heard from those with wealth, power, and privilege. These stories paint a false picture of meritocracy; everyone who works hard can attain wealth, power, and privilege while ignoring the systemic inequalities that institutional racism provides.[17]

Thus, white people are racists simply because they are white and enjoy the privileges of being white in a system that inherently favors whites.

In her book *White Fragility*, DiAngelo says it is so hard for white people to talk about their racism

> **wokeness**
>
> the awareness of systemic oppression and the need for redistribution of power from the oppressor to the oppressed

---

17 "What is Critical Race Theory?" UCLA School of Public Affairs, accessed February 1, 2021, https://spacrs.wordpress.com/what-is-critical-race-theory.

because they simply don't know they are racists—they are blind to it. For viewing and treating blacks and whites the same does not mean, according to DiAngelo, that you're not racist.[18]

Consequently, we are told that whites, especially white men, need to be awakened from their denial. To be woke is to be aware of the inherent and systemic racism, injustices, and inequalities of the capitalistic system in which we live. One activist defines the woke movement as "an encouragement for people to wake up and question dogmatic social norms [a.k.a. traditional values]. It requires an active process of deprogramming social conditionings focusing on consistent efforts to challenge the universal infractions we are all subjected to."[19]

antiracism

the awareness of white people's inability to be non-racists

But and as long as white heterosexual men remain asleep to their racism and homophobia and sexism, they will continue to spread their racism, homophobia, and sexism. "Common sense," DiAngelo claims, "would tell us that because we do not believe in discrimination, we do not engage in it. However, most discrimination is unconscious and takes place whether we intend to

18   See Robin DiAngelo, *White Fragility: Why It's So Hard for White People to Talk About Racism* (Boston: Beacon Press, 2018).
19   "On Wokeness," So You Want to Be Woke, accessed January 8, 2021, https://www.soyouwanttobewoke.com/#about.

discriminate or not, despite genuinely held beliefs in fairness and equity.[20]

True justice, which is *color blindness*, is not the goal of social justice, critical race theory, or Black Lives Matter. In fact, color blindness, where everyone is treated by the same standard regardless of the color of their skin, is the worst form of racism according to liberals like Ibram X. Kendi. In his best-selling book, *How to Be an Antiracist*, he argues, "The most threatening racist movement is not the alt-right's unlikely drive for a White ethno-state, but the regular American's drive for a 'race-neutral' one."[21] This is a long way from Martin Luther King Jr.'s famous assertion that people should not be judged by the color of their skin. By now it should be evident that the goal of social justice is not to change people's hearts or address unjust laws but to create a world where all traces of God's authority have been expunged.

For instance, even married women who are happy to follow God's admonition to be submissive to their husbands and to care for their children at home are not only supposedly oppressed themselves but also contribute to the oppression of others. Though they may be happy, they are restricted. More than that,

20 Sensoy and DiAngelo, *Is Everyone Really Equal?*, 3.
21 Ibram X. Kendi, *How to Be an Antiracist* (New York: Penguin, 2019), 20.

they are propagating this oppression to the next generation—their children. Such women need to feel ashamed of their actions, so say social justice acolytes. And if things continue, their children will need to be removed from such abuse and placed in reeducation camps, as suggested by Michael Beller, the now former principal counsel of the Public Broadcasting Service (PBS).[22] In short, those who don't actively and continuously repudiate the evils of the current ordering of society are aiding oppression and helping it continue on to the next generation. Their silence is violence.

On the other hand, in social justice ideology, reverse racism and reverse sexism are impossible. Blacks can't be racist, and women can't be sexist. Even though they may be biased and prejudiced in their hearts and show partiality in their actions toward white men, they can't be oppressive because they don't wield any institutional power. And even if a black woman heads up a major cooperation that refuses to hire white men, she still can't be racist or sexist because she lives under the broader oppressive capitalistic system.

In sum, there can be no cure to inequality and injustice until communism replaces capitalism and all institutions of power, such as the patriarchal

---

22   Project Veritas, "PBS Principal Counsel Michael Beller Incites Political Violence In Radical Left-Wing Agenda," YouTube, January 12, 2021, https://youtu.be/t1r2rdmWsPE.

family, are replaced with a classless and open society where children are the responsibility of the whole "village." This is the objective behind it all. But a key step in taking down all the delegated authority of God is to "awaken" people from their unawareness of how unjust these institutions of power are.

Control the Narrative and Censor Free Speech

To awaken people from their complacency and their blind acceptance of the current order of things, the third step of Alinsky's plan is to control the narrative by censoring freedom of speech.

As noted in the last chapter, critical theory is founded on the notion that language is oppressive because it is the means of understanding and communicating truth, and the truth is oppressive because it is binding and doesn't care about one's feelings or desires.

Thus, the battle is not with tanks on a battlefield but with liberal textbooks in the schools and universities, progressive ideas in our churches, and censorship of any opposing viewpoints in our news outlets and social media platforms. This fight will be over who controls the narrative being communicated to the masses. Helen Pluckrose and James Lindsay, in their book that critiques critical theory, *Cynical Theories*, explain it this way:

If knowledge is a construct of power, which functions through ways of talking about things, knowledge can be changed and power structures toppled by changing the way we talk about things. Thus, applied postmodernism focuses on controlling discourses, especially by problematizing language and imagery it deems theoretically harmful. This means that it looks for then highlights ways in which the oppressive problems they assume exist in society manifest themselves, sometimes quite subtly, in order to "make oppression visible." The intense scrutiny of language and development of ever stricter rules for terminology pertaining to identity often known as political correctness came to a head in the 1990s.[23]

Saul Alinsky claimed that "radicals must have a degree of control over the flow of events."[24] They must assign blame and quickly use every tragedy, even if it is the lawful and justifiable shooting of a black person by a white police officer, as a tool to control the narrative. In the words of Rahm Emanuel, "Never let a serious crisis go to waste."

The key to controlling the narrative is shaming people into submission. We can lose free speech by brute force or by the fear of being disliked and

23   Helen Pluckrose and James Lindsay, *Cynical Theories: How Activist Scholarship Made Everything about Race, Gender, and Identity—and Why This Harms Everybody* (Durham, NC: Pitchstone, 2020), 61–62.
24   Saul Alinsky, *Rules for Radicals*, 7.

shamed by others. And this is how social justice is turning good into evil and evil into good.

Even now, those who still think homosexuality is an unnatural sin are too scared to voice their opinion out of fear of being labeled as a judgmental, hate-filled Christian. Such an opinion is no longer politically correct. Since the year I was born, 1976, much has changed. Just three years earlier, homosexuality had been declassified as a mental illness, and today, the city where I live, Conway, Arkansas—the buckle of the Bible Belt—has a yearly gay pride parade. On the coattails of this, a push to declassify pedophilia as a mental illness is gaining support. Things are rapidly changing in America. The perversions that once were shameful to even mention are now literally celebrated in the streets, and it is those who would speak against these things that are being shamed.

Because God has written His law in people's consciences and because such sexual perversion goes against nature, those who enjoy such unnatural sexual sins must constantly quiet their guilty consciences by receiving continual affirmation. Since it takes only one voice to confirm their inward guilt, every conservative voice of opposition must be shamed into silence—or eventually stamped out through imprisonment or death.

This new "morality" is not based on the authority of God but on the fallacy that no standard of right and wrong exists. In the minds of the radicals, a person cannot live out their true, inner self until they are wholly unshackled from the old social and conservative constructs of morality. One's inner self—which the Bible calls depravity and Freud called the id—must be free to express itself without guilt or shame.

Relentlessly Assault Resisters

Those who hold to the old conservative values are the ones who are deemed judgmental, intolerant, hateful, and oppressive. Thus Christians—the most loving of people—will be seen as the most intolerant and hateful of people.

Every symbol or word that is viewed as offensive by the interrupter must be labeled as hate speech. Those who continue to voice any traditional values must be canceled. We Christians dare not refuse to bake a cake for a gay wedding,[25] but if a college football coach wears a t-shirt with the logo of a conservative news network, he may just lose his job If an NFL quarterback defends his action of standing for the national anthem, he must be publicly shamed

---

25   John Paul Brammer, "Court rules against Oregon bakers who refused to make gay wedding cake," *NBC News*, December 28, 2017, https://www.nbcnews.com/feature/nbc-out/court-rules-against-oregon-bakers-who-refused-make-gay-wedding-n833321.

on sports networks and social media outlets until he bows to the pressure and retracts all his comments.[26]

Even though many studies have shown that the majority of Native Americans are not offended by sports teams with Indian names and mascots, such as the Washington Redskins,[27] they are to be labeled as oppressive and banned. Despite the family of Aunt Jemima pleading with Quaker not to remove her name and image from their packaging, these have been deemed offensive and therefore must go. Pressure must be placed on the "offending" organizations until they buckle under the endless barrage. If they will not submit to the new standard of morality, retailers must refuse to do business with them until the loss of income forces them to cave.

Now social justice proponents are focusing on the removal of words that define gender, like boy or girl, which they consider to be oppressive. Such terms are designed to pressure boys to act like boys and girls to act like girls. Gender, they say, is merely a social construct designed to keep biological men in power. Masculinity, in their minds, is toxic.

26 Kerry Breen, "Drew Brees faces backlash for saying kneeling during national anthem is disrespectful," *MSN*, June 3, 2020, https://www.msn.com/en-us/sports/nfl/drew-brees-faces-backlash-for-saying-kneeling-during-national-anthem-is-disrespectful/ar-BB14ZJUf.
27 Michael David Smith, "Poll of Native Americans' view of Redskins name finds 'proud' most common answer," *NBC Sports*, August 10, 2019, https://profootballtalk.nbcsports.com/2019/08/10/poll-of-native-americans-view-of-redskins-name-finds-proud-most-common-answer.

A worldview based on the lawlessness of atheism can only tolerate lawlessness. Indeed, all opposing voices must be censored and suppressed until the freedom of speech is taken away. Free speech, you see, is dangerous because, as they claim, language is oppressive. Everything needs to be progressive, fluid, and unbinding. Again, all traces of God's transcendental authority must go for atheism to stand.

The cancel culture will not be content until good is deemed evil and evil is deemed good. Social theorist Jeremy Rifken affirms that this was the real objective all along:

> We no longer feel ourselves to be guests in someone else's home and therefore obliged to make our behavior conform to a set of pre-existing cosmic rules. We make the rules. We establish the parameters of reality. We create the world, and because we do, we no longer feel beholden to outside forces. We no longer have to justify our behavior, for we are now the architects of the universe. We are responsible for nothing outside of ourselves, for we are the kingdom, the power, and the glory forever.[28]

Slowly Centralize Power

Once far-left radicals have been successful at inciting class warfare, demonizing intuitions of power,

---

28 Jeremy Rifkin, *Algeny* (New York: Viking, 1983), 244.

censoring free speech, and relentlessly assaulting resisters, the final step is to provide a solution to cure the world of its oppression. Seeing that power has already been stripped from individuals and families, the state is the only thing left with any authority to effect change.

Because God has been removed from the equation, the state must seek to take His place. Freedoms and rights should be determined and issued by the state. Once power has been taken from the institutions of society, it can supposedly be evenly redistributed to women, blacks, minorities, and other oppressed peoples. For since nature didn't arrange things to be evenly distributed, big government is the only thing that can bring about what Thomas Sowell called "cosmic justice."[29]

You see, this is a war on God, who makes some people tall and some people short. Such inequalities are not fair and just. It is not fair that nature has made some basketball players taller than others or that left-handed people have a harder time finding a pair of scissors than right-handed people or that some people have more money and privileges than others. Nature is just not fair. Privilege is evil.

So because nature is unfair and power and wealth and privileges are not equally distributed, some other

29 Thomas Sowell, *The Quest for Cosmic Justice* (New York: Touchstone, 1999).

authority needs to step in and make things right. In other words, some other power needs to remove God from His temple and do what He chose not to do.

As long as there are separate nations, there will always be a disproportionate distribution of power and wealth among the nations. So, for this new global power to be able to make everything right, it must assume all power. As long as some other delegated power or authority remains in the world, oppression will remain.

Only when a global power that has commandeered all power and authority to itself arises (with all the nations united in their rage against God) will there be social equality. This new power needs to do what God did not do—unify everyone by making everyone identical—unity by uniformity.

Steps toward globalization include a centralized economy, centralized medicine, centralized mass media, centralized transportation, and a centralized military. But again, for this to happen, a slow erosion of individual and national authority must take place for people to willingly turn over their freedoms.

As mentioned in our last chapter, there seem to be three basic ways to strip freedom from people. One, offer to buy their freedom with free stuff. Two, scare people and then offer them security and protection in exchange for their freedom. Three, take it by force.

Offer to Exchange Freedom for Free Stuff

Man's inalienable rights come from God. But such rights stand in the way of Marxism. So, one way in deceiving people into giving up their rights is by offering them a trade. See if they will swap their freedom for free stuff like cell phones and stimulus money. That which only God can give must be exchanged for that which only big government can give—free services, free healthcare, free college education, and other such things. Once people believe the lie that free stuff is a human right, it is much easier to convince them that human rights and freedoms come from big government.

And this changes everything. God designed civil authorities to protect the rights of men, not to give or take them away. But once man believes government is in the place of God and that it is the government's responsibility to provide rather than to protect, then the damage has already been done.

Scare People into Giving Up Their Freedoms

Fear is another thing that leads people to willingly hand over their freedoms. It must be a certain type of fear, however, for some fear, like the worry that a foreign power is going to enslave us, leads people to stand up for their freedoms and fight. But the anxiety that surfaces when we think we will lack basic provisions, like food, water, and medicine, will scare people into giving up their freedom for a sense of security.

Again, people need to be deceived into thinking it's the government's responsibility to provide for, and not just protect them. When natural calamity hits, it is big government's job to fix the problem. When someone loses their job, it's big government's responsibility to pay their lost wages.

With the freedoms God gave His image-bearers comes the responsibility to take dominion and provide for themselves through the work of their own hands. But Marxism reverses this by offering man an exchange of services—give us your God-given freedoms and we make sure you have food on your table and medicine in your cabinet.

Once people believe that health care and handouts are basic human rights, then it is the government who has the right to tell people how to make personal decisions relating to their own health. The government has the right to tax people who make unhealthy decisions. Like Communist China, Big Brother will have the right to monitor your lifestyle and micromanage your decisions. But since people like free things and are scared of going without basic provisions, they are often willing to exchange their God-given freedoms for a bit of free stuff.

Take People's Freedom by Force

The last way of taking individual freedom is the old-fashioned way—by force. Once the majority of people have willingly given up their freedom, it's easier for a nation to silence, imprison, and kill those who refuse to cooperate, such as what is currently going on in China.

Marxism Is a Global Initiative

Karl Marx believed that communism would not be fully functional until the industrial nations of the world were united under the Marxist banner. So, Marx and the Frankfurt School laid out steps to remove power from the local and state level to a national level, and from the national level to the international level.

Along with raising taxes, increasing national debt, and centralizing the banking industry and communication, all forms of nationalism need to be painted as fascist. History must be viewed only through the lens of oppression. Every national sin needs to be highlighted, such as racism, until all national pride turns into national shame. Monuments of national heroes need to be torn down, and historical figures who used to be praised need to be seen as sources of national embarrassment. Schools and military bases need to be renamed. Even Old Glory, the American flag, needs to be reinterpreted from a symbol of freedom to a symbol of oppression and aggression. Kneeling rather than saluting the flag must be seen as the new virtue.

Power needs to be removed from the local police and military. The director of the Frankfurt School, Max Horkheimer, understood that local powers are a threat to centralized power. "There are," Horkheimer said, "a multitude of subtle apparatuses and direct institutions of force (such as police and military) which are working to annihilate such hopes."[30] Thus, we need to be scared into thinking that the police need to be defunded and replaced by social workers and government-trained psychologists.

Marx and Engels and the Frankfurt School outlined the way to slowly implement communism many years ago. And in addition to using the universities as their reeducation and indoctrination centers, governments need to go into deeper debt, raise taxes, and put more and more restrictions on small businesses. To help bring down small businesses, Horkheimer claimed, monopolies need to be created.[31] It will be easier for the government to control a few monopolies than to attempt to simultaneously commandeer hundreds of thousands of small businesses.

---

30 Quoted in Held, *Introduction to Critical Theory*, 45.
31 See Held, *Introduction to Critical Theory*, 53.

Lastly, for there to be a universal and global solution to the problem, there needs to be a global problem to solve. Though science does not validate the theory of manmade global warming, nevertheless, it is propagated as a crisis that can only be combated by a global economic solution. It is not by accident that all global economists root their strategies, like the Green New Deal, in addressing climate change.

A pandemic is also another global crisis that can be capitalized on to promote fear and a global reset to redistribute wealth around the world, as the prime minister of Canada, Justin Trudeau, has suggested.

God calls civil authorities to protect our freedoms from those who seek to do evil and take them away. But once the government seeks to strip the freedoms that God has given to His image-bearers, then the government has become an unjust institution.

A World Religion

As we said at the beginning of this chapter, social justice is Marxism applied. Social justice is the ethical standard of critical theory. But it's not only unjust; it creates the very thing it claims to solve—oppression. Marxism cannot work without taking away our God-given freedoms and bringing us into submission and dependence on big government. It is an atheistic world religion that seeks to replace God with a global state that rules the world with an inverted ethic.

5

THE INTOLERANCE OF SOCIAL JUSTICE

Social justice is the godless religion of Marxists. It is an atheistic attempt to diagnose and solve the world's problems without a divine being, divine truth, and a divine ethic. In addition to misdiagnosing the problem, social-justice-prescribed solutions only bring more injustices, more oppression, and more inequalities.

In a postmodern world, where ultimate meaning does not exist, social justice offers skeptics a bit of purpose. It gives the world some existential meaning and a bit of hope in an otherwise nihilistic worldview. Though it is a false hope, it's still a perceived hope. And this seems to be a reason why social justice is so appealing to postmodernists.

But what is appalling is that social justice has entered through both the back and the front door of the church. The church has the hope of the gospel; thus, it is astonishing that the church is entertaining the claims of social justice. And it is not just liberal churches that have opened the door for social justice to enter. Sadly, many conservative churches have invited it in as well.

Why has the church been so accommodating? The appeal, so it seems to me, is that social justice is the "new morality," and Christians, supposedly, are to support morality wherever they find it. Because Christians don't want to be perceived as judgmental and racist, they buy into the false notion that critical race theory (CRT) is merely an extension of the civil rights movement. Many churches view social justice as compatible with Christianity because they both condemn racism. Because of these perceived common concerns, CRT is welcomed into the church with open arms.

But as we have seen, these concerns are only common in appearance. Like the letter X, Christianity and social justice, though they start at different points, seem to intersect on the subjects of justice and equality. But though they might appear to cross, they have two different foundations (theism and atheism) and two different conclusions (godliness and ungodliness), and upon closer examination, we discover they don't even cross at all.

The apparent overlap is what seems to lure many professing Christians to buy into social justice, but as we have seen, the meanings of justice, equality, and racism are not the same in the social justice worldview as they are in the biblical worldview.

Yet, though Christianity and social justice have nothing in common, some Christians nevertheless fail to see this. Even worse, some Christians who understand the dangers of Marxism still think CRT can be safely used by the church to fight oppression and racism.

Voddie Baucham, in his upcoming book *Fault Lines*, claims that "one of the unintended consequences of the Critical social justice movement is that Christians who adopt its underlying ideologies will not be able to avoid the damage it creates."[1] He shares the sentiments of apologist Neil Shenvi, who says, "The idea that evangelicals can adopt the analysis of contemporary critical theory with respect to race and sex, but not with respect to sexuality, gender identity, or religion is naïve—at best."[2]

The church needs to realize that once individual freedoms are gone, religious freedom will be gone

---

1 Voddie T. Baucham Jr., *Fault Lines: The Social Justice Movement and Evangelicalism's Looming Catastrophe* (Washington, DC: Salem, 2021).

2 Neil Shenvi, "Short Review of Adams' Teachings for Diversity and Social Justice," *Neil Shenvi—Apologetics (blog)*, accessed February 7, 2021, https://shenviapologetics.com/short-review-of-adams-teachings-for-diversity-and- social-justice.

too. Inviting social justice to enter the church is like asking Satan to come and preach and then being surprised afterward that he tried to burn the place down.

Social justice, for the supposed good of the whole, seeks to undermine the authority of the individual, the family, local authorities, and the church. If social justice is fully implemented, no authority but the state will be able to remain in power. The church, as history has shown in every Communist country, like the USSR, Cuba, and China, will be persecuted and suppressed.

Freedom of religion cannot be tolerated because religions like Christianity are deemed oppressive and a part of the old system of morality. Karl Marx made this clear:

> Religion is the sigh of the oppressed creature, the sentiment of a heartless world, and the soul of soulless conditions. It is the opium of the people. The abolition of religion as the illusory happiness of men, is a demand for their real happiness. The call to abandon their illusions is a call to abandon a condition which requires illusions.[3]

In his book *The Principles of Communism*, Engels asks, "What will be its attitude to existing religions?"

---

3 Karl Marx, *Critique of Hegel's 'Philosophy of Right'*, trans. Annette Jolin and Joseph O'Malley (London: Cambridge University Press, 1982), 127.

He goes on to answer, "All religions so far have been the expression of historical stages of development of individual peoples or groups of peoples. But communism is the stage of historical development which makes all existing religions superfluous and brings about their disappearance."[4]

But most significantly, social justice is a counterfeit gospel. Rather than changing the sinful heart—the id—social justice wants to fully unleash it—so that one's perverse sexual desires can be exercised without shame or restraint. Instead of calling out sexual sins, social justice wants to encourage them and make them the norm. In lieu of offering forgiveness to oppressors, social justice wants continual repentance with no forgiveness. Rather than establishing justice, social justice wants to commit injustice by stealing from the Haves to give to the Have Nots. And, lastly, in place of heaven on earth, social justice wants to usher in the godless global tyranny of the state.

Thankfully, God's solution is the real solution to sin, oppression, racism, and injustice. The true gospel not only brings forgiveness, it establishes justice in the death of Jesus Christ. God's law was satisfied at the cross where God's wrath and mercy kissed. By faith in Christ, all sinners without distinction, including oppressors and racists and sexists, can be

---

4 Friedrich Engels, *The Principles of Communism* (N.P.: Pattern Books, 2020), 41, (Question 23).

freely forgiven. The true gospel doesn't restrain the heart of stone but exchanges it for a heart of flesh (Ezek. 36:26). Sinners are set truly free in Christ Jesus. The gospel brings true unity with God and among all those in Christ, where there is neither male nor female or Jew nor Gentile (Gal. 3:28). Finally, only the true gospel will bring restoration to this broken world and establish utopia, which the Bible calls heaven on earth (2 Peter 3:13).

And this unity that is established by God isn't through the elimination of His delegated institutions of power.   Rather, the Bible says it is God who makes some rich and some poor (1 Sam. 2:8), but it is also God, in Christ Jesus, who provides the love and humility needed for the rich and the poor, the powerful and the weak, the Jew and the gentile, the educated and the uneducated, and the master and the slave to walk together in harmony. Only this solution allows for unity in diversity.

The ills of society are not rooted in a disparity of wealth or power or advantages but in a lack of submission to God. Therefore, the world can't fix its problems by throwing away God and His laws. The only way to fix sin is by submitting to the authority of God and looking in faith to Christ.

Because the world is fallen, we thank God that He did not delegate administrative power to only one institution—big government. He has purposefully divided power into four separate jurisdictions: the individual, the family, the state, and the church. May the church be careful to not aid in the undermining of these authorities by embracing social justice.

GLOSSARY

natural revelation — the knowledge that God communicates to man about Himself through nature that is universally and immediately understood by all

nihilism — the philosophical notion that everything, including human life, is meaningless

gaslighting — a manipulation tactic, an attempt to slowly make someone question their own thoughts, perception, or judgment

critical theory — a social philosophy of class warfare that claims language is a social construct used as a means of oppression by those in power and which calls for the deconstruction of power structures through the deconstruction of language

determinism — the philosophical notion that all events are determined completely by the laws of nature that were set in place at the beginning of the cosmos

empiricism — the theory that all knowledge begins and is restricted to that which can be ascertained by sense experience

existentialism — the idea that existence preceeds meaning and purpose

hegemony — the notion, developed by Italian Communist Antonio Gramsci, of a dominant group imposing its own socially constructed values and knowledge onto marginalized groups in order to maintain power over them

patriarchy — the system in which husbands are the leaders of the family and called to take principal roles of leading, providing, and protecting women and children

materialism — the philosophical pre-commitment that all things can be reduced to physical matter

ontology — the branch of philosophy that deals with the nature of being and existence and the relationship between all existing things

epistemology — the branch of philosophy that deals with how knowledge is ascertained

ethics — the branch of philosophy that deals with the relationship between morality and behavior

sin — the transgression of God's law

tabula rasa — the theory that individuals are born without any built-in mental content

hierarchy — the chain of command descending from greater authority to lessor authorities

critical consciousness — the awareness of the power structures that shape and control the world

intersectionality — the idea, developed by Kimberlé Crenshaw, that some individuals, such as black women, are members of multiple oppressed groups who experience multiple layers of oppression, such as racism and sexism

positivism — the notion that science is the foundation of all knowledge

social construction — the notion that norms and values are shaped not by objective truth but by social expectations

systemic power — the controlling influence (i.e., oppression) that is exerted by the institutions of society

antiracism — the awareness of white people's inability to be non-racists

wokeness — the awareness of systemic oppression and the need for redistribution of power from the oppressor to the oppressed

More Books by Free Grace Press

JENNIFER ADAMS
The Gospel Made Clear to Children

NICOLAS ALFORD
Doxology: How Worship Works

SCOTT ANIOL
*Let the Little Children Come: Family Worship on Sunday
(and the Other Six Days Too)*

JOEL BEEKE
Calvin on Sovereignty, Providence, and Predestination
The Christian Teacher as Office-Bearer

JOEL BEEKE AND STEVEN LAWSON
Root & Fruit: Harmonizing Paul and James on Justification

BRIAN BORGMAN
*An Exile's Guide to Walking with God: Meditations on
Psalm 119*
*In Service to the Church: Essays in Honor of
Dr. Robert Paul Martin*

RON CRISP AND DANIEL CHAMBERLIN
Jesus Is Lord: The Mediatorial Reign of Christ

MICHAEL HAYKIN
*Giving Glory to the Consubstantial Trinity:
An Essay on the Quintessence of the Christian Faith*

DON JOHNSON
*Victory in Jesus: A Devotional Commentary on the
Book of Revelation*

JEFFREY JOHNSON
*The Absurdity of Unbelief: A Worldview Apologetic of the
Christian Faith*

Behind the Bible: A Primer on Textual Criticism
The Church (an updated version of The Church: Why Bother?)
The Failure of Natural Theology
The Fatal Flaw of the Theology Behind Infant Baptism
The Five Points of Amillennialism
The Folly of Unbelief
The Gracious Call: Guilt, Justice, & Forgiveness
He Died for Me: Limited Atonement and the Universal Gospel
*The Kingdom of God: A Baptist Expression of Covenant and
    Biblical Theology*
What Every Christian Needs to Know about Social Justice

ALLEN S. NELSON IV
From Death to Life: How Salvation Works

TOM NETTLES
*A Commentary on James: Good Words, Bad Words; Good
    Works, Bad Works; True Faith, False Faith*
Easier for a Camel
The Privilege, Promise, Power, and Peril of Doctrinal Preaching

JIM SCOTT ORRICK
*Seven Thoughts Every Christian Ought to Think Every Day:
    Laying a Foundation for a Life of Prayer*

CHARLES H. SPURGEON
All of Grace, Stephen McCaskell ed.
Spurgeon's Calvinism, Stephen McCaskell ed.
Through the Eyes of Spurgeon, Stephen McCaskell ed.

JOHN AND CINDY RAQUET
*Purposeful and Persistent Parenting: Blessing Others,
    Blue-Tape Boundaries, and Other Practical Perspectives
    on Raising Children*

MICHAEL SEEWALD
Anticipating God's Rest

JEREMY WALKER
On the Side of God: The Life and Labors of Andrew Fuller

JEFFERY SMITH
Preaching for Conversions

KURT M. SMITH
Piety, Passion, Paradox: The Life and Legacy of Basil Manly Sr.
Thundering the Word: The Awakening Ministry of George Whitefield

CAROLYN STALEY
Through the Valley: A Story of Pain, Hurt, and Fear and the Glory of God through It All

SAM WALDRON
The Crux of the Free Offer of the Gospel
Political Revolution in the Reformed Tradition

MODERN REPRINTS
Absolute Predestination, A Modern Reprint, Jerome Zanchius
The Life of God in the Soul of Man, Henry Scougal, modernized by Jeffrey Johnson

BAPTIST REPRINTS
Baptists: Thorough Reformers, John Quincy Adams
A Choice Drop of Honey from the Rock of Christ, Thomas Wilcox
The Glory of a True Church, Benjamin Keach
Plain Christian Duties, Zenas Trivett, with an introduction by Michael Haykin

On Campus & Distance Options Available

GRACE BIBLE
THEOLOGICAL
SEMINARY